The Leadbeater Reader:
A Selection of Occult Essays

By C. W. Leadbeater

Copyright © 2020 Lamp of Trismegistus. All rights reserved. No part of this publication may be reproduced or transmitted in any form or by any means, electronic or mechanical, including photocopying, recording, or by any information storage and retrieval system, without permission in writing from Lamp of Trismegistus. Reviewers may quote brief passages.

ISBN: 978-1-63118-483-3

Esoteric Classics

Other Books in this Series and Related Titles

The Sepher Yetzirah and the Qabalah by M P Hall (978-1-63118-481-9)

The Kabbalah of Masonry & Related Writings by E Levi &c (978-1-63118-453-6)

History, Analysis and Secret Tradition of the Tarot by Hall &c (978-1-63118-445-1)

The Ceremony of Initiation: Analysis & Commentary (978-1-63118-473-4)

Crystal Vision Through Crystal Gazing by Achad (978-1-63118-455-0)

Magical Essays and Instructions by Florence Farr (978-1-63118-418-5)

Ancient Mysteries and Secret Societies by M P Hall (978-1-63118-410-9)

The Secrets of Enoch by Enoch (978-1-63118-449-9)

The Path of Light: A Manual of Maha-Yana Buddhism (978-1-63118-471-0)

The Rosicrucian Chemical Marriage by Christian Rosenkreuz (978-1-63118-458-1)

Qabbalistic Teachings and the Tree of Life by M P Hall (978-1-63118-482-6)

American Indian Freemasonry by A C Parker (978-1-63118-460-4)

The Mysteries of Freemasonry & the Druids by M P Hall &c (978-1-63118-444-4)

Psalms of Solomon by King Solomon (978-1-63118-439-0)

Arcane Formulas or Mental Alchemy by W W Atkinson (978-1-63118-459-8)

The Machinery of the Mind by Dion Fortune (978-1-63118-451-2)

The Gospel of the Nativity of Mary by St. Matthew (978-1-63118-448-2)

Buddhist Psalms by Shinran (978-1-63118-465-9)

Freemasonry and the Egyptian Mysteries by C W Leadbeater (978-1-63118-456-7)

Alchemy in the Nineteenth Century by H P Blavatsky (978-1-63118-446-8)

The Human Aura: Astral Colors and Thought Forms (978-1-63118-419-2)

Audio versions are also available on Audible, Amazon and Apple

Table of Contents

Introduction...7

The Law of Cause and Effect...9

How Clairvoyance is Developed...23

The Influence of Surroundings...41

The Reality of the Astral Plane...49

The Attitude of the Enquirer...71

Why Not I? ...81

Buddhic Consciousness...93

To Those Who Mourn 103

The Hidden Side of Lodge Meetings...123

Masters of Wisdom...131

Ancient Ideals in Modern Masonry...141

INTRODUCTION

The word "esoteric" can be difficult to define. Esotericism in general can be seen less as a system of beliefs and more as a category, which encompasses numerous, different systems of beliefs. It's a bit of juxtaposition, since the word "esoteric" indicates something that few people know about, while the term itself broadly covers numerous philosophies, practices, areas of study and belief systems.

In a greater sense, Esotericism acts as a storehouse for secret knowledge, which is often considered ancient (by *tradition, if not by fact)*, passed down from generation to generation, in private. At various times in history, simply possessing the knowledge of some of these subjects, was considered illegal and a jailable offence, if discovered. This usually included such general topics as Alchemy, Qabalah, Hermeticism, Occultism, Ceremonial Magic, Astrology, Divination, Rosicrucianism and so on. Collectively, these areas of study were often referred to as the esoteric sciences.

Sometimes, the outer garment of a subject isn't esoteric, while what is hidden beneath it, is. As an example, Freemasonry isn't necessarily esoteric by nature (at *least not anymore)*, but certain signs, passwords and handshakes given to the candidate during their initiation, are in fact, esoteric, in the sense that they are hidden from the general public.

Today, in the twenty-first century, such topics are readily available at bookstores across the country, and numerous mainsteam publishers offer beginners guides and coffee-table volumes on many of these subjects, intended for mass appeal. Books like *"The Secret"* have turned previously arcane topics into household knowledge. All that being the case, however, it isn't to say that there still aren't buried secrets to uncover, ancient wisdom being ignored and forgotten mysteries to be explored. In fact, it is often that we are only able to further our own studies by standing on the shoulders of these disappearing giants.

Lamp of Trismegistus is doing its part to help preserve humanity's esoteric history by making some of these classics available to those students who are seeking to unearth the knowledge of these ancient colossi.

So, be sure to check other titles from our *Esoteric Classics* series, as well as our *Occult Fiction, Theosophical Classics, Foundations of Freemasonry Series, Supernatural Fiction, Paranormal Research Series, Studies in Buddhism* and our *Christian Apocrypha Series*. You can also download the audio versions of most of these titles from Audible, Amazon and Apple, for learning on the go.

THE LAW OF CAUSE AND EFFECT

I have explained elsewhere that what we usually call man's life is simply one day in the real and larger life, and that when what we call death comes to him he simply lays himself down to sleep at the conclusion of his life day. You will see very readily that the benefit to be derived from this scheme of development in successive lives is contingent upon the continued existence of the same great general laws. It is only because the great Law of Divine Justice is always the same, that the experience gained in one incarnation is useful in the next. So that belief in this law of cause and effect is in fact an integral part of the doctrine of reincarnation. Its influence in reality is even more far-reaching than the next physical life; it extends also into the after-death condition, and a full comprehension of its working is of the greatest importance to us.

As to this law of divine justice, there have been various opinions at various times. Some people; when they have looked out into the world, and seen what was happening, have wondered whether there was a law of justice at all. I do not deny that from a purely physical point of view we are sometimes unable fully to see the action of this great law. Yet I know that it exits, and that when we do not see its working the fault lies in our own blindness, and not in the action of the law. We may be quite certain that the law exists, and yet be fully prepared to admit that it is not always possible for us down here to see the whole of its working. Although I put this law before you as a hypothesis for your consideration, it is much more than a hypothesis for those who are studying from the Theosophical standpoint. Very many of them know by the use of faculties beyond the physical that reincarnation is a definite fact. In the same way there are very many students who know certainly that this law of cause and effect is in action. But we must realize that this law is working itself out upon other planes besides the physical, and so is not to be gauged only from one point of view. Suppose we were looking at the underside of some very beautiful tapestry; you will comprehend that, being only able to see the underside, we should have a very imperfect idea of the pattern. Suppose, further that the tapestry had not been finished, then still less should we be able to form a clear conception of the design. That is precisely how we stand with regard to the mighty law of karma. We only see the underside of it from the physical plane because so much of its action belongs to higher levels. Indeed, we might expect scarcely ever to be able to trace it fully from this side. Once more, as in the case of reincarnation, if you will provisionally accept this idea of divine justice, you will find that it is a more satisfactory theory of life than any other, and you may gradually come to hold it as firmly as we do.

You will observe that there are only certain hypotheses. Either everything is only blind chance, and we are ruled by caprice, or we are under a regular divine law, and our surrounding are the result of our actions, good or evil, in previous lives. You will admit that you would like to believe in a law of divine justice. There must be a reason for that feeling that man has of always desiring justice. If God is infinitely greater than we, He must surely have this quality. We believe in Theosophy that it is a rational necessity that this law should exist, and we see in every direction instances of its workings. I can explain it only to a limited extent, because it needs long and careful study. But the broad outline we ought to be able to give, and then the details can be gathered from the literature. Never think that when you have heard a lecture on a Theosophical subject you know all about it. You have only to take up some of our books to see how very much more there is to be known, for in one lecture it is not possible to give all available information even on one point.

The first great characteristic that I should like you to grasp about this law is that it is automatic in its action, and that therefore there is no possibility of escape from it. Put aside all theories that man will be judged for his actions, and punished or rewarded for them. That inevitably suggests to us the thought of an earthly judge, who may be prejudiced or partially informed, or may be more lenient in one case and more severe in another. We prefer rather to speak of the law of cause and effect, because we hold that this is a law which brings us the result of our actions with an automatic precision. In mechanics we know that action and reaction are equal, and that no force can ever be lost, and we find that precisely the same rule obtains on these higher levels. If you put so much energy into a machine, you will receive back from it so much work as a result. If you put a certain amount of energy into a word, deed, or thought, you will obtain from that also a certain result, for the law of the conservation of energy holds good upon higher planes just as it does upon this.

If you put a certain amount of force into a steam-engine, you expect to get a definite proportion back in the shape of work - not all of it, naturally, because some goes in friction and some is thrown off in the form of heat, but still a fair proportion. If you do not receive back from your engine what you know you may reasonably expect, you at once look for a defect in your machine; it would never occur to you to say that the law of the conversation of energy is false. But when exactly the same law is working on higher planes, people who find an individual instance in which they cannot see that evil flows from evil and that good follows good, seem often to affirm wildly that no law of justice exists, instead of blaming themselves for their own short-sightedness, or tranquilly realizing that we cannot expect always to see how this law works out in results, because they are not always immediate, and the time occupied may often extend far beyond our physical purview. Often forces set in motion in one life have not time to work themselves out in that incarnation or even in the next, but they will inevitably be worked out some time. We are, today, to a large extent, the products of the thoughts, surroundings, and the teachings of our childhood, even though the details of that life may be forgotten. Just as today we are bearing the results of yesterday, and the day before, so precisely is it with the larger day, the incarnation. We have made ourselves what we are, and we have made our circumstances what they are. As we have sown in the past, so are we reaping now; and as we are sowing now, so infallibly shall we reap in the future.

It is especially important to emphasize the truth that this Divine Law is inexorable, because a good deal of the religious teaching of the present day distinctly includes a theory we may escape from the consequences of our actions. In Theosophy we consider that a very dangerous doctrine, not only because it is fundamentally inaccurate, but because of the many unsound conclusions which are deduced from it. The idea suggested is that by doing wrong the man has simply incurred a debt, and that this debt may just as well be paid by someone else as by the sinner himself - or rather that the sinner cannot himself pay, and so must shuffle off his responsibility. This simile of the debt is one that we have sometimes employed in Theosophical writing, but it seems to me liable to very serious misunderstanding. A much truer analogy would be that of a man who wishes to be an athlete and is training himself for a race. In order to acquire sufficient strength and agility he must develop certain muscles, and for that purpose he needs a certain training. It would not at all serve that purpose if someone else did it for him. If we wish to become perfect men physically we must take much trouble to develop those parts of the body which we have hitherto neglected, and we must rest others which we have over worked. The physical condition of the average man is no inapt symbol of his moral condition. Many muscles are almost atrophied for want of use, while other parts of the body - the nervous system, for instance - have been seriously injured by improper use. From the standpoint of the physical we have committed many sins against our own bodies, and we must atone for them; if we want to become perfect men physically we must go through many wearisome exercises and trials, which would not have been necessary if we had kept our bodies properly and evenly develop. Others can help us, by telling us what to do and how best to do it, but others cannot take the exercise for us. It is not like the liquidation of a debt, because in addition to bearing the result of wrong done in the past, the man must in bearing it develop strength for the future. He must develop perfect moral qualities in the same way as he would develop perfect muscles - by exercising them. He must make the necessary effort to put things right again. No one else can do it for him, but happily many may help him by advice and sympathy and affectionate encouragement. This law of cause and effect works just as do other laws of Nature, and if we can recognize that it will save us much trouble. If you put your hand into the fire, and it is burnt, you do not say "God punished me for putting my hand into the fire". You consider it a natural consequence of your action, and you know that anyone who understands physics could explain to you along scientific lines exactly what had happened to you, and why you suffered. He would tell you that incandescent matter is vibrating at an exceedingly rapid rate, that such a rate of vibration impinging upon the tissues of your hand had torn them apart, and so had produced the wound that we call a burn. But there is no special Divine interposition in that, though it takes place under the operation of those laws of Nature which are the expression of the Divine Will on the physical plane.

We hold that sorrow and suffering flow from sin just precisely in that way, under the direct working of natural law. It may be said, perhaps, that obviously the good man does not always reap his reward of good result, nor does the wicked man always suffer. Not always immediately; not always within our ken; but assuredly eventually and inexorably. If we could see the future, if we could even see the whole of the present, we should understand this fully. We shall see more clearly that this must be so if we define exactly what we mean by good and evil. Our religious brothers would tell us that that was good which was in accordance with God's will, and that that was evil which was in opposition to it. The scientific man would say that that was good which helped evolution, and whatever hindered it was evil. Those two men are in reality saying exactly the same thing; for God's will for man is evolution, and when that is clearly realized all conflict between religion and science is at once ended. Anything, therefore, which is against the evolution of humanity as a whole is against the divine will. We see at once that when a man struggles to gain anything for himself at the expense of others he is distinctly doing evil, and it is evil because it is against the interest of the whole. Therefore the only true gain is that which is a gain for the race as a whole, and the man who gain something without cost or wrong to anyone is raising the whole race somewhat in the process. He is moving in the direction of evolution, while the other man is moving against it.

Take a simple illustration. Suppose that I have here a great weight suspended from the ceiling by a rope. If I exert a certain force in pushing against this weight, we know by the laws of mechanics that it pushes back against my hand with exactly the same amount of force. We find that that same law of mechanics holds good on the higher planes just as it does here. If a man exerts his strength against the Divine order, he disturbs the equilibrium of nature, and that equilibrium infallibly readjusts itself at the expense of the man who disturbs it. The power of the current of the Divine will is so much greater than that of any human will which may attempt to deflect it that it sweeps him inevitably on, and it is only he who suffers, not the Divine scheme. He cannot delay the current, but he may cause a little temporary disturbance and foam upon its surface. He is swept along with it in any case, but he can go on in two ways. He can intelligently observe its direction and swim with it, and by doing so he will not only progress with ease and comfort himself, but will also (which is much more important) be able to extend a helping hand to others. On the other hand, he may set himself against it, through a foolish misunderstanding of his own interests. He will still be carried on in spite of his struggles, but with a great deal of trouble and pain to himself, and perhaps of hindrance to others also. That is precisely what the wicked man is doing. He will be swept along more slowly and with a great deal of sorrow and suffering for himself and others, but he must evolve.

If we can grasp the grand idea that there is no possibility of final destruction, but the certainty of final success for all, because that is God's will for them, we shall at once recognize the utter futility and madness of selfishness. There is no feeble hope that a few may be saved, but the magnificent certainty that none can by any possibility be lost.

I have sometimes wondered how modern orthodoxy can speak of Christ as the Savior of the world, and yet in the same breath assert that He does not save it, that He does not succeed in saving one in ten thousand of its inhabitants, and has to yield all the rest to the Devil! Would that be considered a successful effort if we were speaking of any kind of human attempt? Such a doctrine is a blasphemy; cast it out from your stock of religious ideas. We bring a grander gospel and we preach a nobler creed than that; for we know that this evolution will succeed and not fail

- that it will be a grand and glorious success, and that every soul in it shall eventually attain its goal.

It is only the ignorant who struggles, and even he must yield in the end. He will struggle against the evolutionary current in one life - perhaps even in more than one, but his soul will learn its lesson, will observe the inevitable connection between cause and effect, and will strive to control its vehicles more efficiently. Let us see a little how this works. In the first lecture I mentioned the planes of nature, and explained that man had bodies corresponding to them. We have to remember that this law of cause and effect is acting with regard to those planes as well as to this. If the man has strong emotions, those represent forces which are producing their effect in the astral body. If he has good mental development, that represents a force belonging to his mental body, which is inevitably producing results also.

Suppose a man finds himself what we call an emotional person, easily swayed either by feeling of affection or by annoyance. That man has an emotional nature, a readily impressible astral body which he brought over from a previous life. He need not, however, carry it on with him to another. A man who finds himself and train himself definitely with a view to the future. If he lets himself go and allows his passion to dominate him, he encourages his astral body to indulge in those violent vibrations, he sets up a habit in it which becomes every time more difficult to conquer. If, on the other hand, he sets himself to try to curb his anger, he gradually gets those vibrations under his control, and each time it is a little easier than before. It often happens that a man who is irritated says something which he afterwards regrets. He resolves not to do this again, but when the next provocation comes, he does not remember in time; perhaps for several more times he will pull himself up just as he has spoken the angry word. But there comes a time when he remembers in the very act of speaking and checks himself abruptly, and then his victory is half won. Presently he stops himself just before he speaks the word, and then he has won the victory as far as the physical plane is concerned, though he has still to go on and control the feeling itself - to prevent even the vibration in the astral body. That is the way in which a man learns to break through a bad habit.

Fortunately we may set up good habits as readily as bad ones, if we will only take the trouble. We may try definitely to set up within ourselves good habits of helpfulness, unselfishness, perseverance, punctuality, and so on; and then we shall be born with these as inherent qualities upon our next return to earth. That is a little bit of character-building which anyone may undertake, and the trouble it costs him will be the best investment he ever made. When we understand that the mental body and astral body are only expressions of the man, we shall realize that in learning to control them he is acquiring definite qualities and building them into the causal body, so that next time he will have those qualities as part of his stock-in-trade, as it were, with which he recommences his business of evolution. The man sows certain thoughts and actions, and later on he reaps the results. Between the spring sowing and the autumn reaping he many have worn out one suit of clothes and put on another in the shape of a new body, but he remains the same and he reaps his harvest just the same.

We find by investigation that, broadly speaking, the man's thoughts in one life build his character for the next, and that his actions in the one life produce his surrounding in the next. A strong desire along certain lines which remains entirely unfulfilled during one life will often produce a capacity along those lines in the next. For example, I have known people who are very musical in the sense that they enjoy music intensely, but yet have no faculty for producing it, no facility in performance and no opportunity for acquiring it, although they earnestly wish for it. Now that strong desire will certainly produce its results in the next incarnation. Assuredly those people will next time bring back with them the capacity for musical training, and will have the opportunity for it. They will not be born with the training already acquired, as Mozart was, he must have had that training in his previous life; but at least it will bring them back with a vehicle which will readily respond to the training. Thus aspirations or desires of one life are transmuted into capacities in the next.

Just so if the man is constantly thinking some thought over and over again, he sets up a habit or tendency of thought. Whenever a man thinks strongly he creates a thought-form - that is to say, he sets up a certain rate of vibration, and the energy thus generated draws round itself a vehicle of finer matter which it ensouls, and thus creates a sort of storage battery of force. Now that thought-form hovers about the man and constantly reacts upon him. We know from telepathic experiments what is the tendency of a thought when it acts upon another person. It will work upon the corresponding matter of his matter body and tend to set up in that its own rate of vibration, so that it provokes in the mind of the recipient a reproduction of the thought which was in the mind of the sender. That would be the action on another person; but we often forget that a man is constantly producing a very similar action on himself. Clairvoyants see every man surrounded by a cloud of his habitual thoughts, and of course these thoughts are all the while reacting upon him. To every man there come times when he is not thinking strongly, when for the moment his mental activities are in abeyance; and at all such times ever present thought-forms would react upon him, so that any strong thought which the man has once sent forth will always tend to reproduce itself and make him think a similar thought whenever his mind is for the moment vacant.

You can see how this might work in the case of a sensualist, and how very likely the man would be to yield to such a returning thought because he has been in the habit of giving way to similar impressions before. The man himself sent out the idea in the first place, and perhaps has never thought of it since, but when the opportunity occurs it reacts upon him. So it may become a sort of tempting demon like those invented by the diseased imagination of medieval monks. Most unfortunately it may act upon others as well as upon himself, and that is the awful responsibility of yielding to evil thought. He may become the center of moral contagion and do grievous harm to thousands of whose very existence he is ignorant.

Again, if a man dwells often upon a certain thought it will presently translate itself into action. By thinking it so often he sets up a decided tendency, and if circumstances prevent him from carrying it out in action in this life, he will probably do so in his next incarnation. Thus it is that we find some children born with criminal tendencies, with an apparently instinctive desire to steal or to be cruel - because they indulged in covetous or revengeful thoughts in the dim distance of the past. Happily the same law holds with regard to good thoughts. How often we long to do some good deed, but from lack of means or time or strength we are utterly unable to accomplish it. Yet the earnest desire is not without its effect and the opportunity which is denied to us in this life, because our past was not such as to deserve it, will assuredly be ours in the future, won for us by the very energy poured out in the yearning of today.

Along the very same lines is conscience built up in the man. He does a wrong or foolish act, and through the inevitable action of the law he suffers for it sooner or later, and through that very suffering the soul acquires the knowledge that that action is wrong, and must not be repeated. Thus out of painful experiences the conscience in man is formed, the soul learning perhaps a different lesson in each of its lives, and so gradually developing a comprehensive and educated conscience. Usually he cannot impress upon his physical brain the detailed history of his previous mistake not the reason for his conclusion; but he is able to send through very definitely that conclusion itself, in the shape of a firm conviction that a certain action is to be avoided.

It is necessary to realize that we have all of us had many lives, not only one or two; and that since we have gradually raised ourselves to this level, those previous incarnations were all probably less advanced in many ways than our present one. We must all have been savages in the past - and probably not once, but many times. So we must have done a great many evil and undesirable things, and we must each one of us have a tolerably heavy bill to pay. So there arises the question how we are to clear off such an accumulation of evil results. In such lives as the more thoughtful among us are living now, we may reasonably hope that there

HOW CLAIRVOYANCE IS DEVELOPED

When a man has studied the subject of clairvoyance sufficiently to realize that the claims made on its behalf are true, his next enquiry usually is "How can I gain this power for myself? If this faculty be latent in every man, as you say, how can I so develop myself as to bring it into motion, and so have direct access to all this knowledge of which you tell me?" In reply we can assure him that this thing can be done, and that it has been done. There are even many ways in which the faculty may be gained, though most of them are unsafe and eminently undesirable, and there is only one that can be thoroughly and unreservedly recommended to all men alike. But that we may understand the subject, and see where lie the dangers that have to be avoided, let us consider exactly what it is that has to be done.

In the case of all cultured people belonging to the higher races of the world, the faculties of the astral body are already fully developed, as I have explained in earlier lectures. But we are not in the least in the habit of using them; they have slowly grown up within us during the ages of our evolution, but they have come to us so gradually that we have not as yet realized our powers, and they are still to a great extent untried weapons in our hands. The physical faculties, to which we are thoroughly accustomed, overshadow these others and hide their very existence, just as the nearer light of the sun hides from our eyes the light of the far-distant stars. So that there are two things to be done if we wish to enter into this part of our heritage as evolved human beings; we must keep our too-insistent physical faculties out of the way for the time, and we must habituate ourselves to the employment of these others, which are as yet unfamiliar to us.

The first step, then, is to get the physical senses out of the way for the present. There are many ways of doing this, but broadly they all range themselves under two heads - one comprising methods by which they are forced out of the way by temporary violent suppression, and the other including methods, much slower, but infinitely surer, by which we ourselves gain permanent control over them. Most of the methods of violent suppression are injurious to the physical body, to a greater or less extent, and they all have certain undesirable characteristics in common. One of these is that they leave the man in a passive condition, able perhaps to use his higher senses, but with very little choice as to how he shall employ them, and to a large extent undefended against any unpleasant or evil influence, which he may happen to encounter. Another characteristic is that any power gained by these methods can at best be only temporary. Many of them confer it only during the limited period of their action, and even the best of them can only dower the man with certain faculties during this one physical life. In the East, where they have studied these matters for so many centuries, they divide methods of development into two classes, just as I have done, and they call them by the names laukika and lokothra, the first being the "worldly" or temporary method, any results gained by which will inhere only in the personality, and therefore by available only for this present physical life, while whatever is obtained by the second process is gained by the ego, the soul, the true man, and so is a permanent possession for evermore, carried over from one earthly life to another. For most methods of the former class little training is required, and when there is training it is of the vehicles only, and so at the best it can affect only this present set of vehicles, and when the man returns into incarnation with a fresh set all his trouble will be lost; whereas by the second method it is the soul itself which is trained in the control of its vehicles, and naturally it can apply the power and the knowledge thus gained to its new vehicles in the next life. Let me mention to you first some of the undesirable ways in which clairvoyance is developed in various countries.

Among non-Aryan tribes in India it is often obtained by the use of drugs - bhang, hashish, and others of the same kind. These stupefy the physical body something as anesthetics do, and thus the man in his astral vehicle is set free as he would be in sleep, but with far less possibility of being awakened. Before taking the drug, the man has set his mind strongly on the endeavor to train his astral senses into activity, and so as soon as he is free he tries to use his faculties, and with practice he succeeds to some extent. When he awakens his physical body, he remembers more or less of his visions, and tries to interpret them, and in that way he often obtains a great reputation for clairvoyance and prevision. Sometimes while in his trance, he may be spoken through by some dead man, just as any other medium may be. There are others who obtain the same condition by inhaling stupefying fumes, usually produced by the burning of a mixture of drugs. It is probable that the clairvoyance of the pythonesses of old was often of this type. It is stated in the case of one of the most celebrated of those oracles of ancient days, the priestess sat always upon a tripod over a crack in the rock, out of which vapor ascended. After breathing this vapor for a time, she became entranced, and some one then spoke through her organs in the ordinary way so familiar to the visitors to séances. It is not difficult for us to see how undesirable both these methods are from the point of view of real development.

Probably most of us have heard of the dancing dervishes, one part of whose religion consists in this curious dance of ecstasy, in which they whirl round and round in a kind of frenzy until vertigo seizes them and they eventually fall insensible to the ground. In that trance, worked up as they are by religious fervor, they frequently have most extraordinary visions, and are able to some extent to experience and remember lower astral conditions. I have seen something of this, and also of the practices of the Obeah or Voodoo votaries among the Negroes; but these latter are usually connected with magical ceremonies, loathsome, indecent, horrible, such as none of us would dream of touching for any purpose, whatever results might be promised to us. Yet they certainly do produce results under favorable conditions, though not such results as any of us could possibly wish to obtain. Indeed, none of the methods mentioned so far would at all commend themselves to us, though I have heard of Europeans who have experimented with the Oriental drugs.

Nevertheless we also have undesirable methods in the West - methods of self-hypnotization, which should be carefully avoided by all who wish to develop in purity and safety. A person may be told to gaze for some time at a bright spot, until paralysis of some of the brain centers supervenes, and in that way he is cast into a condition of perfect passivity, in which it is possible that the lower astral senses may come into a measure of activity. Naturally he has no power of selection in receiving under such circumstances; he must submit himself to whatever comes in his way, good or bad - and on the whole it is much more likely to be bad than good. Sometimes the same general result is obtained by the recitation of certain formulae, the repetition of which over and over again deadens the mental faculty almost as the gazing at a metal disc does. It may be remembered that the poet Tennyson tells us that he was able by the recitation of his own name many times in rapid succession to pass into another condition of consciousness. The account is given in a letter in the poet's handwriting, which is dated Faringford, Freshwater, Isle of Wight, May 7th, 1874. It was written to a gentleman who communicated to him certain strange experiences he had when passing from under the effect of anesthetics. Tennyson says:

> *"I have never had any revelations through anesthetics; but a kind of waking trance (this for lack of a better name) I have frequently had, quite up from boyhood, when I have been all alone. This has often come upon me through repeating my own name to myself silently, till all at once out of the intensity of the consciousness of individuality, the individuality itself seemed to dissolve and fade away into boundless being; and this not a confused state, but the clearest of the clearest, the surest of the surest, utterly beyond words, where death was an almost laughable impossibility, the loss of personality (if so it were) seeming no extinction, but the only true life. I am ashamed of my feeble description. Have I not said the state is utterly beyond words? This is the most emphatic declaration that the spirit of the writer is capable of transferring itself into another state of existence, is not only real, clear, simple, but that it is also infinite in vision and eternal in duration."*

Now here is undoubtedly a touch of the higher life; no one who has practical experience of realities can fail to recognize the description as far as it goes, even though the poet just stops short on the brink of something so infinitely grander. He seems to have held himself more positive than do many people who dabble in these matters without the necessary instruction or knowledge, and so he gained a valuable certainty of the existence of the soul apart from the body; yet even his method cannot be commended as good or really safe.

We are sometimes told that such a faculty can be developed by means of exercises, which regulate the breathing, and that this plan is one largely adopted and recommended in India. It is true that a type of clairvoyance may be developed along these lines, but too often at the cost of ruin both physical and mental. Many attempts of this sort have been made here in the United States; I know it personally, because on my previous visit many who had ruined their constitutions and in some cases brought themselves to the verge of insanity came to me to know how they could be cured. Some have succeeded in opening astral vision sufficiently to feel themselves perpetually haunted; some have not even reached that point, yet have wrecked their physical health or weakened their minds so that they are in utter despair; some one or two declare that such practice has been beneficial to them. It is true that such exercises are employed in India by the Hatha Yogis - those who attempt to attain development rather by physical means than by inner growth of the mental and the spiritual. But even among them such practices are used only under the direct orders of responsible teachers, who watch the effect upon the pupil of what is prescribed, and will at once stop him if the exercises prove unsuitable for him. But for people who know nothing at all of the subject to attempt such things indiscriminately is most unwise and dangerous, for practices which are useful for one man may very well be disastrous for another. They may suit one man in fifty, but they are extremely likely not to suit the rest, and myself I should advise every one to abstain from them unless directed to try them by a competent teacher who really understands what they are intended to achieve. You may be the one man whom they will suit, but the probabilities are against it, for there are far more failures than successes. It is so fatally easy to do a great deal of harm in this way, that to experiment vaguely is rather like going into a chemist's shop and taking down drugs at random; you might happen to hit upon exactly what you needed, but also you might not, and the latter is many times more probable.

Another method by which clairvoyance may be developed is by mesmerism - that is to say, if a person be thrown by another into a mesmeric trance, it is possible that in that trance he may see astrally. The mesmerizer entirely dominates his will, and the physical faculties are thrown utterly into abeyance. That leaves the field open, and the mesmerist can at the same time stimulate the astral senses by pouring vitality into the astral body. Good results have been produced in this way, but it requires a very unusual combination of circumstances, an almost superhuman development of purity in thought and intention both in the operator and the subject to make the experiment a safe one. The mesmerist gains great influence over his subject - a far greater power than is generally known: and it may be unconsciously exercised. Any quality of heart or mind possessed by the mesmerist is very readily transferred to the subject, so if he be not entirely pure, we see at once that avenues of danger open up before us. To be thrown into a trance is to give up your individuality, and that is never a good thing in psychic experiments; but beyond and above that element of undesirability there is real danger unless you have the highest purity of thought, word and deed in your operator; and how rarely that is to be found you know as well as I do. I should never myself submit to this process; I should never advise it to anyone else.

I say nothing against the practice of curative mesmerism by those who understand it; that is a totally different matter, for in that it is unnecessary to produce the trance condition at all. It is perfectly possible to relieve pain, to remove disease, or to pour vitality into a man by magnetic passes, without "putting him to sleep" at all. To this there can be no possible objection; yet the man who tries to do even this much would do well to acquaint himself thoroughly with the literature of the subject, for there must always remain a certain element of danger in playing, even with the noblest intentions, with forces which you do not understand, which to you are still abnormal forces. None of these are plans of clairvoyant development, which can be unreservedly recommended for trial by everyone.

What, then, it may be asked, are the desirable methods, since so many are undesirable? Broadly, those which instead of suppressing the physical body by force, train the soul to control it. The surest and safest way of all is to put oneself into the hands of a competent teacher, and practice only what he advises. But where is the qualified teacher to be found? Not, assuredly among any who advertise themselves as teachers; not among those who take money for their instruction, and offer to sell the mysteries of the universe for so many shillings or so many dollars. Knowledge can be gained now where it has always been available - at the hands of those who are adepts in this great science of the soul, the fringe of which we are beginning to touch in our deepest studies. There has always been a great Brotherhood of the men who know, and they have always been ready to teach their lore to the right man, for it is for that very purpose that they have taken the trouble to acquire it, in order that they may be able to guide and help. How can we reach them? You cannot reach them in the physical body, and you might not even know them if it should happen to you to see them. But they can reach you, and assuredly they will reach you when they see you to be fit for the work of helping the world. Their one great interest is the furthering of evolution, the helping of humanity; they need men devoted to this work, and they are ever watching for them; so none need fear that he can be overlooked if he is ready for that work. They will never gratify mere curiosity; they will give no aid to the man who wishes to gain powers for himself alone; but when a man has shown by long and careful training of himself, and by using for helpfulness all the power that he already possesses, that his will is strong enough and his heart pure enough to bear his part in the divine work - then he may become conscious of their presence and their aid when he least expects it.

It is true that they founded the Theosophical Society, yet membership in the Society will not of itself be sufficient to bring a man into relationship with them - no, nor even membership in that inner

School through which the Society offers training to its more earnest members. It is true that from the ranks of the Society men have been chosen to come into closer relation with them; but none could guarantee that as a result of becoming a member, for it rests with them alone, for they see further into the hearts of men than we. But always be sure of this, you whose hearts are yearning for the higher life, for something greater than this lower world can give, that they never overlook one honest effort, but always recognize it by giving through their pupils such teaching and such help as the man at his stage is ready for.

In the meantime, while you are trying in every way to develop yourselves along the path of progress, there is much that you can do, if you wish, to bring this power of clairvoyance nearer within your reach. Remember that it is not in itself a sign of great development; it is only one of the signs, for man has to advance along many lines simultaneously before he can reach his goal of perfection. See how highly developed is the intellect in the great scientific man; yet perhaps he may have but little yet of the wonderful force which devotion gives. See the splendid devotion of the great saint of some Church or religion; yet in spite of all that progress along one line he may have but little yet of the divine power of the intellect. Each needs what the other has, each will have to acquire the faculty of the other before he will be perfect, So it is evident that at present we are unequally developed! Some have more in one direction, and some in another, according to the line along which each has worked most in past lives. So if you particularly long for devotion in your character, by striving in that direction now you may attain much of it even in this life, and may assuredly make it a leading quality in your next life. So with intellect, so with every quality; so also with this faculty of clairvoyance. If you think it well to throw your strength into work along this line, you may do very much towards bringing these latent faculties into action. I am not speaking here of a vague possibility, but of a definite fact, for some of our own members in this Society set themselves years ago to try to train the soul along the path of permanent progress, and of those who persevered without faltering almost everyone has even already found some definite result. Some have won their faculties fully, others only partially as yet, but in all cases good has come from their efforts to take themselves in hand and control their minds and emotions.

If you have this desire for higher sight, take yourself in hand first in the same way; make sure first of the mental and moral development, lest you should succeed in your efforts, and gain your powers. For to possess them without having first acquired those other qualifications would be indeed a curse and not a blessing, for you would then misuse them, and your last state would indeed be worse than the first. If you consider that you have made sure of yourself, and you can trust yourself under all possible circumstances to do the right for the right's sake, even against your earthly seeming interest, always to choose the utterly unselfish course of action, and to forget yourself in your love for the world, then there are at least two methods which will leads you towards clairvoyance safely, and can in no way do you harm, even though you should not succeed in your object. The first of these, though perfectly harmless and even useful, is not suited for everyone, but the second is of universal application, and I have myself known both of them to be successful.

This first method is a purely intellectual one, a study to which I have already on several occasions had to refer, the study of the Fourth Dimension of space. The physical brain has never been accustomed to act at all along those lines, and so it feels itself unable to attack such a problem. But the brain, like any other part of the physical organism, can be trained by persistent, gradual, careful effort to feats which appeared originally quite beyond its reach, and so it can be induced to understand and conceive clearly the forms of a world unlike its own. The chief apostle of the Fourth Dimension is Mr. C. H. Hinton, of Washington, D.C. He is not a member of our Society, but he has done many of its members an excellent piece of service in writing so clearly and luminously on his wonderful subject. In his books he tells us that he has himself succeeded in developing this power of higher conception in the physical brain, and several of our own members have followed in his footsteps. One of these has developed astral sight simply by steadily raising the capacity of the physical brain until it contained the possibility of grasping astral form, and thus awakening the latent astral faculty proper. It is simply a question of extending the power of receptivity until it includes the astral matter. But I suppose that out of a score of men who took up this study, not more than one would succeed as well and as quickly as that; but at any rate the study is a most fascinating one for those who have a mathematical turn of mind, and where it does not bring increased faculty to see, it must at least bring wider comprehension and a broader outlook over the world, and this is no mean result, even if no other be attained. Short of absolute astral sight, it is the only method of which I know by which a clear comprehension can be gained of the appearance of astral objects, and thus a definite idea of what the astral life really is.

If that line of effort commends itself only to the few, our second method is of universal application. It also is not easy, but its practice cannot but be of the greatest use to the man. That is its great and crowning advantage; it leads a man towards these powers which he so ardently desires; but the rate at which he can move along that road depends upon the degree of his previous development in that particular way in other lives, and therefore no one can guarantee him a certain result in a certain time; yet while he is working his way onward, every step which he takes is so far an improvement, and even though he should work for the whole of his life without winning astral sight, he would nevertheless be mentally and morally and even physically the better for having tried. This is what in various religions is called the method of meditation. For the purpose of our examination of it I shall divide it into three successive steps: concentration, meditation and contemplation, and I will explain what I mean by each of these three terms.

But remember always that to attain success, this effort must be only one side of a general development, and that it is absolutely prerequisite for the man who would learn its secrets to live a pure and altruistic life. There is no secret about the rules of the greater progress, the Steps of the Path of Holiness have been known to the world for ages, and in my little book "Invisible Helpers" I have given a list of them according to the teaching of the Buddha, with the characteristics which mark each of its stages. There is no difficulty in knowing what to do, the difficulty is in carrying out the directions which all religions have given.

The first step necessary towards the attainment of the higher clairvoyance is concentration - not to gaze at a bright spot until you have no mind left, but to acquire such control over your mind that you can do with it what you will, and fix it exactly where you want to hold it for as long a period as you choose. This is not an easy task, it is one of the most difficult and arduous known to man, but it can be done, because it has been done - not once, but hundreds of times, by those whose will is strong and immovable. There may be some among us who have never thought how much beyond our control our minds usually are. Stop yourself suddenly when you are walking along the street, or when you are riding in the car, and see what you are thinking, and why. Try to follow the thought back to its genesis, and you will probably be surprised to find how many desultory thoughts have wandered through your brain during the previous five minutes, just dropping in and dropping out again and leaving almost no impression. You will gradually begin to realize that in truth all these are not your thoughts at all, but simply cast-off fragments of other people's thoughts. The fact is that thought is force, and every exertion of it leaves an impression behind. A strong thought about some other person goes to him, a strong thought of self-clings about the thinker; but so many thoughts are not by any means strong or especially pointed in any direction, and so the forms which they create are vaguely-floating and evanescent. While they last they are capable of entering into any mind that happens to come their way, and so it comes that as we walk along the road we leave a trail of feeble thought behind us, and the next man who passes that way finds these valueless fragments intruding themselves upon his consciousness. They drift into his mind, unless it is already occupied with something definite, and in the majority of cases they just drift out again, having made only the most trifling impression upon his brain; but here and there he encounters one which interests or pleases him and then he takes that up and turns it over in his mind, so that it departs from him somewhat strengthened by the addition of a little of his mind-force to it.

He has made it his own thought for a moment, and so has colored it with his personality. Every time we enter a room we step into the midst of a crowd of thoughts, good, bad or indifferent as the case may be, but the great mass of them just a dull, purposeless fog, which is hardly worth calling thought at all.

If we wish to develop any higher faculty, we must begin by gaining control over this mind of ours. We must give it some work to do, instead of just letting it play about as it will, drawing into itself all those thoughts which are not ours, which we really do not want at all. It must be not our master but our servant before we can take the first step along the line of the true trained clairvoyance, for this is the instrument, which we shall have to use, and it must be at our command and fully under our control.

This concentration is one of the hardest things for the ordinary man to do, because he has had no practice at it, and indeed has scarcely realized that it needed to be done. Think what it would be if your hand were as little under your control as your mind is, if it did not obey your command, but started aside from what you wished it to do. You would feel that you had paralysis, and that your hand was useless. But if you cannot control your mind, that is dangerously like a mental paralysis; you must practice with it until you have it in hand and can use it as you wish. Fortunately concentration can be practiced all day long, in the common affairs of everyday life. Whatever you are doing, do it thoroughly, and keep your mind on it. If you are writing a letter, think of your letter and of nothing else until it is finished; it will be all the better written for such care. If you are reading a book, fix your mind on it and try to grasp the author's full meaning. Know always what you are thinking about, and why; keep your mind at intelligent work, and do not leave it time to be so idle, for it is in those idle moments that all evil comes.

Even now you can concentrate very perfectly when your interest is sufficiently keenly excited. Then your mind is so entirely absorbed that you hardly hear what is said to you or see what passes round you. There is a story told in the East about some skeptical courtiers, who declined to believe that an ascetic could ever be so occupied with his meditation as to be unaware that an army passed close by him as he sat under his tree wrapped in thought. The king, who was present, assured them that he would prove to them the possibility of this, and proceeded to do so in a truly Oriental and autocratic way. He ordered that some large water-jars should be brought and filled to the brim. Then he instructed the courtiers each to take one and carry it; and his command was that they should walk, carrying this water, through the principal streets of the city. But they were to be surrounded by his guards with drawn swords, and if one of them spilled one single drop of his water, that unfortunate was to be instantly beheaded then and there. The courtiers started on their journey filled with terror; but they all got safely back again, and the king smilingly greeted them with a request to tell him all the incidents of their walk, and describe the persons whom they had met. Not one of them could mention even one person that they had seen, for all agreed that they had been so entirely occupied with the one idea of watching the brimming jars that they had noticed nothing else of any sort. "So, gentlemen", rejoined the king, "you see that when there is sufficient interest concentration is possible."

When you have attained concentration such as that, not under the stress of the fear of instant death, but by the exertion of your will, then you may profitably try the next stage of effort. I do not say that it will be easy, on the contrary, it is very difficult; but it can be done, for many of us have had to do it. When your mind is thus an instrument, try what we call meditation. Choose a certain fixed time for yourself, when you can be undisturbed; the early morning is in many ways the best, if that can be managed. It is not always an easy time for us now, for we have in modern civilization hopelessly disarranged our day, so that noon is no longer its middle point, as it should be. Now we lie in bed long after the sun has risen, and then stay up injuring our eyes with artificial light long after he has set at night. But choose your time, and let it be the same time each day, and let no day pass without your regular effort. You know if you are trying any sort of physical exercise for training purposes how much more effective it is to do a little regularly than to make a violent effort one day, and then do nothing for a week. So in this matter it is the regularity that is important.

Sit down comfortably where you will not be disturbed, and, turn your mind, with all its newly-developed power of concentration upon some selected subject demanding high and useful thought. We in our Theosophical studies have no lack of such subjects, combining deepest interest with greater profit. If you prefer it, you can take some moral quality, as is advised by the Catholic Church when it prescribes this exercise. In that case, you would turn the quality over in your mind, see how it was an essential quality in the Divine order, how it was manifested in Nature about you, how it had been shown forth by great men of old, how you yourself could manifest it in daily life, how *(perhaps)* you have failed to display it in the past, and so on. Such meditation upon a high moral quality is a very good exercise in many ways, for it not only trains the mind but keeps the good thought constantly before you. But it needs to be preceded generally by thought upon concrete subjects, and when those are easy for you, you can usefully take up the more abstract ideas.

When this has become an established habit with you, with which nothing is allowed to interfere; when you can manage it fairly well without any feeling of strain or difficulty, and without a single wandering thought venturing to intrude itself; then you may turn to the third stage of our effort - contemplation. But remember that you will not succeed with this until you have entirely conquered the mind-wandering. For a long time you will find, when you try to meditate, that your thoughts are continually going off at a tangent, and you do not know it till suddenly you start to find how far away they have gone. You must not let this dishearten you, for it is the common experience; you must simply bring the errant mind back again to its duty, a hundred or a thousand times if necessary, for the only way to succeed is to decline to admit the possibility of failure. But when you have at length succeeded, and the mind is definitely mastered, then we reach that for which all the rest has been but the necessary preparation, good though it has also been in itself.

Instead of turning over a quality in your mind, take the highest spiritual ideal that you know. It does not matter what it is, or by what name you call it. A Theosophist would most probably take one of those Great Ones to whom we have already referred - a member of that great Brotherhood of Adepts, whom we call the Masters - especially if he had the privilege of having come directly into contact with one of them. The Catholic might take the Blessed Virgin or some patron saint; the ordinary Christian would probably take the Christ; the Hindu would perhaps choose Krishna, and the Buddhist most likely the Lord Buddha himself. Names do not matter, for we are dealing with realities now. But it must be to you the highest, that which will evoke in you the greatest feeling of reverence, love and devotion that you are capable of experiencing. In place of your previous meditation, call up the most vivid mental image that you can make of this ideal, and, letting your most intense feeling go out towards this highest One, try with all the strength of your nature to raise yourself towards Him, to become one with Him, to be in and of that glory and beauty. If you will do that, if you will thus steadily continue to raise your consciousness, there will come a time when you will suddenly find that you are one with that ideal as you never were before, when you realize and understand Him as you never did before, for a new and wonderful light has somehow dawned for you, and all the world is changed, for now for the first time you know what it is to live, and all life before seems like darkness and death to you as compared with this.

Then it will all slip away again, and you will return to the light of common day - and darkness indeed will it appear by comparison! But go on working at your contemplation, and presently that glorious moment will come again and yet again; and each time it will stay with you longer, till there comes a period when that higher life is yours always, no longer a flash or a glimpse of paradise, but a steady glow, a new and never-ceasing marvel every day of your existence. Then for you day and night will be one continuous consciousness, one beautiful life of happy work for the helping of others; yet this, which seems so indescribable and so unsurpassable, is only the beginning of the entrance into the heritage in store for you and for every child of man. Look about you with that new and higher sight, and you will see and grasp many things which until now you have never even suspected - unless, indeed you have previously familiarized yourself with the investigations of your predecessors along this path.

Continue your efforts, and you will rise higher still, and in due course there will open before your astonished eyes a life as much grander than the astral as that is than the physical, and once more you will feel that the true life has been unknown to you until now; for all the while you are rising nearer to the One life which alone is perfect Truth and perfect Beauty.

This is a development that must take years, you will say. Yes, that is probable, for you are trying to compress into one life the evolution, which would normally spread itself over many; but it is far more than worth the time and the effort. No man can say how long it will take in any individual case, for that depends upon two things - the amount of crust that there is to break through, and the energy and determination that is put into the work. He could not promise you that in so many years you would certainly succeed; he can only tell you that many have tried before you, and that many have succeeded. All the great Masters of Wisdom were once men at our own level; as they have risen, so must we rise. Many of us in our humbler way have tried also, and have succeeded, some more and some less, but none who has tried regrets his attempt, for whatever he has gained, be it little or much, is gained for all eternity since it inheres in the soul which survives death. Whatever we gain thus we possess, in full power and consciousness, and have it always at our command; for this is no mediumship, no feeble intermittent trance-quality, but the power of the developed and glorified life which is to be that of all humanity someday.

But the man who wishes to try to unfold these faculties within himself will be very ill-advised if he does not take care first of all to have utter purity of heart and soul, for that is the first and greatest necessity. If he is to do this, and to do it well, he must purify the mental, the astral and the physical; he must cast aside his pet vices and his physical impurities; he must cease to defile his body with meat, with alcohol or tobacco, and try to make himself pure and clean all through, on this lower plane as well as on the higher ones. If he does not think it worth giving up petty uncleanness for the higher life, that is exclusively his own affair; it was said of old that one could not serve God and Mammon simultaneously. I do not say that bad habits on the physical plane will prevent him altogether from any psychic development, but do very emphatically and distinctly say that the man who remains unclean is never free from danger, and that to touch holy things with impure hands is to risk a terrible peril. The man who would try for the higher must free his mind from worry and from lower cares; while doing his duty to the uttermost, he must do it impersonally and for the right's sake, and leave the result in the hands of higher powers. So will he draw round him pure and helpful entities as he moves onward, and will himself radiate sunlight on those in suffering or in sorrow. So shall he remain master of himself, pure and clean and unselfish, using his new powers never for a personal end, but ever for the advancement and the succor of men his brothers, that they also, as they can, may learn to live the wider life, may learn to rise from amid the mists of ignorance and selfishness into the glorious sunlight of the peace of God.

THE INFLUENCE OF SURROUNDINGS

Influence is perpetually radiated upon us by all objects of Nature, even by the very earth upon which we tread. Each type of rock or soil has its own special variety, and the differences between them are very great, so that their effect is by no means to be neglected. In the production of this effect three factors bear their part: the life of the rock itself, the kind of elemental essence appropriate to its astral counterpart, and the kind of nature-spirits which it attracts.

The point for us to bear in mind is that each kind of soil—granite or sandstone, chalk, clay or lava—has its definite influence upon those who live on it, an influence that never ceases. Night and day, summer and winter, year in and year out, this steady pressure is being exercised, and it has its part in the molding of races and districts, types as well as individuals. All these matters are as yet but little comprehended by ordinary science. But there can be no doubt that in time to come these influences will be thoroughly studied, and the doctors of the future will take them into account and prescribe a change of soil as well as of air for their patients.

An entirely new and distinct set of influences is brought into play wherever water exists, whether it be in the form of lake, river, or sea— all of them truly powerful in different ways, but most powerful and observable in the last. Here also the same three factors have to be considered: the life of the water itself, the elemental essence pervading it, and the type of nature-spirits associated with it.

Very strong influences are also radiated by the vegetable kingdom; the different kinds of plants and trees vary greatly in their effect. Those who have not specially studied the subject invariably underrate the strength, capacity, and intelligence shown in vegetable life. Trees, especially old trees, have a strong and definite individuality, well worthy the name of a soul. This soul, though temporary in the sense that it is not yet a reincarnating entity, is nevertheless possessed of considerable power and intelligence along its own lines. It has decided likes and dislikes, and to clairvoyant sight it shows quite clearly by a vivid rosy flush, an emphatic enjoyment of the sunlight and the rain, and undoubted pleasure also in the presence of those whom it has learnt to like, or with whom it has sympathetic vibrations. Emerson appears to have realized this, for he is quoted in Hutton's *Reminiscences* as saying of his trees: "I am sure they miss me; they seem to droop when I go away, and I know they brighten and bloom when I go back to them and shake hands with their lower branches."

It must be remembered that an old forest tree is a very high development of vegetable life, and that when it is transferred from that kingdom it will not pass into the lowest form of animal life. In some cases its individuality is even sufficiently distinct to allow it to manifest itself temporarily outside its physical form, and in that case it will often take the human shape... *Omne ignotum pro magnifico*; and if primitive man saw a huge grave human form come forth from a tree, he was likely enough in his ignorance to set up an altar there and worship it, not in the least understanding that he himself stood far higher in evolution than it did, and that its very assumption of his image was an acknowledgement of that fact.

The occult side of the instinct of a plant is also exceedingly interesting. Its one great object is always to found a family and reproduce its species; and it certainly has a feeling of active enjoyment in its success, in the color and beauty of its flowers and in their efficiency in attracting bees and other insects. Unquestionably plants feel admiration lavished upon them and delight in it; they are sensitive to human affection and they return it in their own way.

When all this is borne in mind, it will be readily understood that trees exercise much more influence over human beings than is commonly supposed. Those who choose to cultivate sympathetic and friendly relations with *all* their neighbors, vegetable as well as animal and human, may both receive and give a great deal of which the average person knows nothing, and may thus make their life fuller, wider, more complete.

The classification of the vegetable kingdom adopted by the occultist follows the line of the seven great types, and each of these is divided into seven sub-types: a set of temperamental characteristics, which it never wholly loses. Although in order to express itself it needs matter belonging to all the different types, it will still have a preponderance of its own type, and will always recognizably belong to that type and no other, until after its evolution is over when it returns to the Logos as a glorified spiritual power through the same channel by which it originally rushed out as a mere undeveloped potentiality.

The distinction between the magnetism radiated by the oak and the pine, the palm tree and the banyan, the olive and the eucalyptus, the rose and the lily, the violet and the sunflower, cannot fail to be obvious to any sensitive person. Wide as the poles asunder is the dissimilarity between the "feeling" of an English forest and a tropical jungle, or the bush of Australia or New Zealand.

For thousands of years humans have lived so cruelly that all wild creatures fear and avoid them, so the influence of the animal kingdom upon humanity is practically confined to that of the domestic animals. In our relations with domestic animals our influence over them is naturally far more potent than theirs over us, yet this latter is by no means to be ignored. People who have really made friends with an animal are often much helped and strengthened by the affection lavished upon them in return. Being more advanced, human beings are naturally capable of greater love than an animal is, but the animal's affection is usually more concentrated, and it is far more likely to throw the whole of its energy into it than a person is. The very fact of the human being's higher development gives them a multiplicity of interests, among which their attention is divided; the animal often pours the entire strength of his nature into one channel, and so produces a most powerful effect. People have a hundred other matters to think about, and the current of their love consequently cannot but be variable. When the dog or the cat develops a really great affection it fills the whole of their life, and they therefore keep a steady stream of force always playing upon their object—a factor whose value is by no means to be ignored. Similarly the individual who is so wicked as to provoke by cruelty the hatred and fear of domestic animals becomes by a righteous retribution the center of converging forces of evil. It must be remembered that such conduct arouses deep indignation among nature-spirits and other astral and etheric entities, as well as among all right-minded people, whether living or dead.

Since it is emphatically true that no person can afford to be disliked or feared by their cat or dog, it is clear that the same consideration applies with still greater force to the human beings that surround us. It is not easy to overestimate the importance of winning the kindly regard of those with whom we are in constant association—the value to a teacher of the attitude towards him of his pupils, to a merchant of the feeling of his clerks, to an officer of the devotion of his men—and this entirely apart from the obvious effects produced on the physical plane. If a person holding any such position as these is able to arouse the enthusiastic affection of their subordinates, they become the focus upon which many streams of such forces are constantly converging. Not only does this greatly uplift and strengthen them, but it also enables them—if something of the working of occult laws is understood—to be of far greater use to those who feel the affection, and to do much more with them than would otherwise be possible.

It should be observed that to obtain this result, it is not in the least necessary that there should be uniformity of opinion. As to the particular effect with which we are at present concerned, mental attitudes have no connection whatever; rather, it is a matter of strong, kindly feeling. If the feeling should unfortunately be of an opposite kind—if the person is feared or despised—currents of evil influence are perpetually flowing towards them, which cause weakness and discord in the vibrations of their higher vehicles, and also cuts them off from the possibility of doing satisfactory and fruitful work with those under their charge.

It has been said that we are known by the company we keep. It is also to a very large extent true that we are *made* by it, for those with whom we constantly associate are all the while unconsciously influencing us and bringing us by degrees more and more into harmony with such vibrations as they radiate. Those who are much in the presence of a large-minded and unworldly individual have a very fine opportunity of becoming large-minded and unworldly themselves, for a steady though imperceptible pressure in that direction is perpetually being exerted upon them, so that it is easier for them to grow in that way than in any other. For the same reason, a person who spends his time loafing with the idle and vicious is exceedingly likely to end by becoming idle and vicious himself. The study of the hidden side of things emphatically endorses the old proverb that "evil communications corrupt good manners."

This fact of the enormous influence of close association with a more advanced soul is well understood in the East, where it is recognized that the most important and effective part of the training of a disciple is that they shall live constantly in the presence of the teacher and bathe in his or her aura. The various vehicles of the teacher are all vibrating with a steady and powerful swing at rates both higher and more regular than any which the pupil can yet maintain, though he may sometimes reach them for a few moments; but the constant pressure of the stronger vibrations of the teacher gradually raises those of the pupil into the same key. A person who has as yet but little musical ear finds it difficult to sing correct intervals alone, but if they join with another stronger voice, which is already perfectly trained, the task becomes easier—which may serve as a kind of rough analogy. The great point is that the dominant note of the teacher is always sounding, so that its action is affecting the pupil night and day without need of any special thought on the part of either of them. Growth and change must of course be ceaselessly taking place in the vehicles of the pupil, as in those of all other human beings; but the powerful vibrations emanating from the teacher render it easy for this growth to take place in the right direction, and exceedingly difficult for it to go any other way, somewhat as the splints which surround a broken limb ensure that its growth shall be only in the right line, so as to avoid distortion.

No ordinary human being, acting automatically and without intention, will be able to exercise even a hundredth part of the carefully directed influence of a spiritual teacher. But numbers may to some extent compensate for lack of individual power, so that the ceaseless though unnoticed pressure exercised upon us by the opinions and feelings of our associates leads us frequently to absorb many of their prejudices without knowing it. Therefore it is distinctly undesirable that we should remain always among one set of people and hear only one set of views. It is eminently necessary that we should know something of other viewpoints, for only in that way can we learn to see good in all. Only by thoroughly understanding both sides of any case can we form an opinion that has any right to be called a real judgment. The biased person is always and necessarily the ignorant person; and the only way in which that ignorance can be dispelled is by getting outside of our own narrow little circle, and learning to look at things for ourselves and see what they really are—not what those who know nothing about them suppose them to be.

The extent to which our human surroundings influence us is only realized when we change them for a while. The most effective method of doing this is to travel in another country. But true travel is not rushing from one large hotel to another, consorting all the time with one's own people and grumbling at every custom that differs from ours. It is rather to live for a time quietly in some foreign land, trying to really get to know its people and to understand them; to study a custom and see why it has arisen, and what good there is in it, instead, of condemning it offhand because it is not our own. The traveler who does this will soon come to feel the characteristic influences of the various races—to comprehend such fundamental diversities as those between the English and the Irish, the Indian and the American, the Breton and the Sicilian, and yet to realize that they are to be looked upon not as one better than another, but as the different colors that go to make up the rainbow, the different movements that are all necessary as parts of the great oratorio of life.

The ordinary tourist is too often imprisoned in the triple armor of aggressive race- prejudice; they are so full of conceit over the supposed excellences of their own nation that they are incapable of seeing the good in any other. The wise traveler who is willing to open their heart to the action of higher forces may receive from this source much that is valuable, both of instruction and experience. But in order to do that they must begin by putting themselves in the right attitude; they must be ready to listen rather than to talk, to learn rather than to boast, to appreciate rather than to criticize, to try to understand rather than rashly to condemn.

We know how often travel is recommended as a cure for many physical ills, especially for those which manifest themselves through the various forms of nervous derangement. Most of us find it to be fatiguing, yet also undeniably exhilarating, though we do not always realize that this is not only because of the change of air and of the ordinary physical impressions but also because of the change of the etheric and astral influences which are connected with each place and district. Ocean, mountain, forest or waterfall, each has its own special type of life, astral and etheric as well as visible; and, therefore, its own special set of impressions and influences. Many of these unseen entities are pouring out vitality, and in any case the vibrations, which they radiate, awaken unaccustomed portions of our etheric double, and of our astral and mental bodies. The effect is like the exercise of muscles which are not ordinarily called into activity—somewhat tiring at the time, yet distinctly healthy and desirable in the long run.

City-dwellers are often accustomed to their surroundings, and usually do not realize the horror of them until they leaves them for a time. To dwell beside a busy main street is, from the astral point of view, like living on the brink of an open sewer: a river of fetid mud, which is always throwing up splashes and noisome odors as it rolls along. No human being, however unimpressionable, can endure this indefinitely without deterioration, and an occasional change into the country is a necessity on the ground of moral as well as physical health. In traveling from the town into the country, we also leave behind us to a great extent the stormy sea of waning human passion and labor, and such human thoughts as still remain to act upon us are usually of the less selfish and more elevated kind. In the presence of one of Nature's great wonders, such as Niagara Falls, almost everyone is temporarily drawn out of themselves and out of the petty round of daily care and selfish desire, so that their thought is nobler and broader, and the thought-forms which they leave behind them are correspondingly less disturbing and more helpful. These considerations once more make it evident that in order to obtain the full benefit of travel a man or woman must pay attention to Nature and allow it to act upon them. If they are wrapped up all the while in selfish and gloomy thoughts, crushed by financial trouble, or brooding over their own sickness and weakness, little benefit can be derived from the healing influences.

To take a walk in the country is to travel on a smaller scale, and in order to appreciate its healthful effect we must bear in mind what has been said of all the different vibrations issuing from various kinds of trees or plants, and even from different kinds of soil or rock. All these act as a kind of massage upon the etheric, astral and mental bodies, and tend to relieve the strain which the worries of our common life persistently exert upon certain parts of these vehicles. Glimpses of the truth on these points may sometimes be caught from folk traditions. For example, there is a widely spread belief that strength may be gained from sleeping under a pine tree with the head to the north. For some cases this is suitable, and the rationale of it is that there are magnetic currents always flowing over the surface of the earth, which are quite undetected by most people. These magnetic currents, by steady, gentle pressure, gradually comb out the entanglements and strengthen the particles both of the astral body and of the etheric part of the physical, thus bringing them more into harmony and introduce rest and calm. The part played by the pine tree is first that its vibrations make the person sensitive to those magnetic currents, and bring that person into a state in which it is possible for them to act upon him, and secondly, that it is constantly throwing off vitality in that special condition in which it is easiest for a person to absorb it.

THE REALITY OF THE ASTRAL PLANE

To speak about the astral plane in India is a somewhat different thing from speaking about it in other lands. In England or in America the great difficulty which the ordinary auditor finds with regard to the matter is to believe that there is any condition beyond the physical. Although the religion of those countries teaches quite as decidedly (*although not as accurately*) as yours that there is another state of existence, a state after death, yet unfortunately the statements made about it by their churches and in their sacred books are put in such an unscientific manner that the trend of modern thought (*which is, as you know, along more or less precise and scientific lines*) leads people practically to reject all that is said about the unseen world. Again and again I have lectured on such subjects in many places; again and again newspaper editors, in commenting upon what I have said, have remarked that it was most reasonable, that in every way it seemed exactly what it ought to be - and yet they invariably concluded by saying, "But of course it is absolutely impossible that anybody really can know anything about these matters." In fact, they seem to think that although Theosophical teaching may be what they call in Italy, well invented, it cannot really mean anything or be anything more than a brilliant hypothesis.

Now I take it that that is not in the least the difficulty which will beset an Indian audience with regard to this matter. You all know from ancient teaching that there is an unseen world - that there is very much existing about us and acting about us all the time, of which our physical senses bring us no report whatever. You are all aware of that, and you do not need any further proof of it; or if there should be any of you who do, they must be the products of half-assimilated western education. There are, however, some difficulties in the minds of many Hindus with regard to the astral plane and the Theosophical teaching concerning it. I have met at different times with two classes of objections in this country, and I should like to say a word about them.

Should the Astral Plane be Studied?

First, it is considered by some Indians that although the astral plane exists, it is yet a thing about which we should think as little as possible. There is such a place, of course, and we must pass through its conditions, but our duty is to fix our thoughts upon the very highest ideal that we can reach, to strain upwards towards that, and not to contemplate any of these lower and intermediate conditions. With part of that I perfectly agree. It is true that every man should set before himself constantly the highest ideal which he is capable of forming. It is unquestionably well that his thoughts should be aimed at that ideal, and that it should influence him in all his actions and through the whole course of his life. But we have this to remember. We are here in the physical world and our duty at the present moment is largely connected with that world. We are in this physical body precisely in order that we may learn lessons through it. If we had no lessons to learn on this material level, we should already have transcended it and we should not need any further incarnation here. So it cannot be argued that in keeping before ourselves the highest ideal we ought to ignore life on the physical plane.

You may say that to some extent the hermit does ignore this lower world, but that is not the usual course. If a man's karma be such that he can legitimately tear himself away from everything physical and go away and live in a cave or in a jungle and devote himself utterly to the contemplation of the highest, that man is already in the fortunate position of being able largely to leave the physical plane out of his calculations. But you all know well that for the enormous majority of you such a way as that is not possible. You may be just as highly developed or as good as the hermit, but you have plain and obvious duties which nothing would justify your discarding. That being so, it is clear that some knowledge of the physical world is of value to you. A teacher who told you to keep your mind fixed only on Nirvanic conditions and to learn nothing about the surroundings of daily life and the temptations which you may meet, would manifestly not be a practical guide.

I should submit, in answer to the objection which I mentioned to you at the beginning, that for the great majority of us a certain amount of life upon the astral plane is a necessity for our evolution. If we have not yet transcended the physical, still less have we transcended this higher realm of Nature, and it is inevitable that many of us should have considerable experiences in connection with the astral plane. Remember that we pass at least one-fourth of our lives, and in many cases one-third, in the sleep of the physical body, and that during that time the consciousness of the man is not asleep, but is active in another vehicle and on another plane of matter. A condition in which we spend at least one quarter of our life is hardly one that is well for us entirely to ignore; and we must also remember that after casting aside our physical bodies we shall most of us pass some considerable time in this astral world, so that it cannot be entirely unimportant to know what we may with regard to it.

There is yet another consideration. Many of us are trying to utilize some powers a little higher than the physical, such as the power of thought, and the power of strong, loving, helpful emotion. If these are to be used efficiently, some knowledge of the material through which they work is required - some knowledge of the conditions under which they are to be employed. I do not say that without such knowledge it would be impossible to produce any result, but I do say that it would be achieved somewhat blindly and that much of the effort would be wasted; whereas with some comprehension of the laws of this higher side of our world it is less likely that strength will be squandered uselessly and valuable time lost. In order that we may help forward the evolution of the world while our physical bodies are in a state of rest, or after they have been cast aside, we must have some knowledge of the subject. It is true that there are certain fascinations connected with the astral world - possibilities of selfishness and sensuality of various kinds; and those who enter upon astral life may quite conceivably be entangled in such snares, and thus delayed in their progress. But each many will necessarily have some contact with astral life whether he knows anything about it or not; and the more he knows about it, the better he understands it, the more likely will he be to avoid mistakes.

Never for one moment have any of our writers suggested to any person that he should set before him astral life as a goal at which to aim. We have consistently said, "Always set the very highest before you as the goal; but since you have to live on the physical plane, recognize the fact and try to understand that, after all, the physical world also is a manifestation of the Supreme, that the astral world is simply nothing but the continuation of the physical world in finer matter, and that you may study the astral conditions of matter precisely as you study etheric conditions of matter, by applying to them scientific methods of research." That is the way in which we have been approaching this matter, both in writing and in lecturing; and I do not think that any Indian who really understands our attitude will take exception to it.

Is Our Description Accurate?

Another objection which I have heard in India is of a different character. There are many Indian teachers who know of the existence of the astral plane, but they say that the accounts of it which they find in Theosophical books do not agree with their own experiences of it. That is a legitimate objection, and it is quite easy for us from our standpoint to understand the position of the man who makes it; but I think that from his standpoint he cannot find it easy to understand our position unless he supposes us the victims of some kind of gigantic hallucination. Now undoubtedly a man may become a victim of illusion, and he may carry on for a long time the same line of illusions, and may live among the thought-forms thus created; and a scheme resting upon the vision of a single person might quite conceivably be accounted for in this way. But while I at least have never asked any human being to believe anything because I have seen it or because I know it, I do think that what has been written in Theosophical literature with regard to the astral plane and to the life and work upon that plane is very fairly well established, by reason of the fact that that is the nearest plane in consciousness to the physical, and that, therefore, we have a considerable number of persons who have had at least occasional experiences in connection with it, and a smaller number for whom it is a prominent part of regular daily life, to whom it is just as familiar as are the streets of your city to you.

If you speak of statements concerning some very high plane which only a few have as yet been able to touch in consciousness, then naturally you have for them so much the less of testimony, for that plane is necessarily much further removed from the physical, and therefore fewer experiments have been made in connection with it. In that case an objector would have more justification in holding that perhaps there might be errors in matters so far beyond ordinary consciousness. But when we are dealing with a band of investigators, people of different races, of varying temperaments and types, and when, in spite of all these differences, they broadly agree as to what they see and how they see it, when they constantly meet in that condition of consciousness, the memory of which is often transferred to the physical plane on opposite sides of the world, it will be readily understood that for those people themselves there grows to be a strong conviction that they are not hallucinated when they believe themselves to be using a consciousness somewhat more extended than that of the average man, and they are consequently quite undisturbed by the criticism of men who have not studied the subject. Those of us who have enquired into the matter have a huge mass of evidence that the astral plane is a reality and that clairvoyance is a fact, and that by means of this faculty we have gained much information which we have put before our brothers in order that they may also have the benefit which such knowledge has brought to us.

I have heard it said here in India that no one ought to give a lecture or write a book on these subjects until he has attained Adeptship, because short of that there must be imperfection. That is quite true; but I would suggest that if our revered founder, Madame Blavatsky, had followed that advice and had waited for the attainment of perfect Adeptship before writing anything, we should not have had "The Secret Doctrine". If Mrs Besant, Mr Sinnett and others had adopted that plan we should have had no Theosophical books for perhaps six or seven thousand years yet, and while the books would undoubtedly have been far more valuable when they came, still the present generation would not have gained the advantage of Theosophical teaching.

We have chosen deliberately to put the imperfect knowledge before our brothers, because we have always felt that such powers come to us not for ourselves only but for them - that we are, so to speak, eyes for our fellows, and we have tried to be faithful eyes. We have tried to report exactly what we have seen, even though we know far better than others what are the difficulties that lie in the way of an accurate report. We know well that you will have very much more to learn as the years roll on, but what we have tried to do, though we may not have wholly succeeded, is to put these things before you in such a manner that as your perceptions widen you will have nothing to unlearn - you will have only to add to your stock of knowledge, and not to alter it. What I think we may hope is that we leave no fundamental principles wrongly stated.

If we consider carefully the astral experiences of many of our Indian friends, and also of some Christian mystics, we shall see that they may readily be harmonized with our own, even though at first sight they seem to differ. It should be remembered that the astral world is as extensive and as varied as the physical world. If visitors from some other planet were to come to this earth and carry back to their own their reports of what they had seen here, it is obvious that twenty of them, or indeed fifty or a hundred of them, might visit different parts of this world, and carry back with them widely differing stories, even though all of them reported accurately the experiences through which they had passed. Exactly in the same way the person who visits the astral plane comes into contact only with a very small part of it, and unless he constantly repeats his visits, and makes systematic efforts to investigate all its varied possibilities, he will naturally return with an exceedingly partial report.

It often happens that by intensity of devotion a man is able to raise his consciousness to the astral level. He forms a strong mental image of the object of his devotional feeling and surrounds himself by a shell that keeps away all other thoughts or vibrations. Thus, even when his consciousness acts through his astral vehicle, it still acts within that shell, and so he sees nothing but the object of his devotion, and is as entirely unaware of the varied life and activity which surrounds him as the ascetic who sits in rapt meditation is unmindful of movements taking place in the physical world around him. We who work on the astral plane constantly see men thus in ecstasy within their own private holy places, created by the intensity of their devotion; and undoubtedly they derive the greatest benefit from such experiences. But they err when they assume that the whole astral world is included in their shell, and that there is nothing to be found there but that which they have seen. This it will be obvious that while their theory of this world of subtle matter leaves them no alternative but to suppose us hallucinated, our theory has the advantage of fully including and explaining their experiences without suggesting any such unpleasant insinuation.

Its Agreement with the Scriptures

You will observe that in speaking of this subtler world I am using the term "astral plane", and not "Kamaloka", which is often employed as a Sanskrit equivalent. I avoid that because I am not sure that it is an equivalent, for I think that when you define it as the place of desire you mean almost exclusively lower desire, and that would make it much more limited than is the astral plane. I believe that your term "bhuvarloka" is much nearer to a correspondence, but without an exhaustive study of references I dare not pledge myself even to that. The way in which the Indians approach the subject, and the way in which their books are written, are somewhat the reverse of ours. They always descend upon it from above, as it were, and their great Rishis, scheming out the whole plan of the universe, say with the calm certainty of knowledge "Thus it must be".

We, on the other hand, approach the subject from below, and patiently catalogue fact after fact over and over again, venturing to draw our deductions only after comparing the results of varied and oft-repeated experiments and observations. But the point which I think should be of interest to you in India is that although these investigations are made from so different a direction, the results agree precisely with the statements of your ancient books, thus offering a corroboration of the religious teaching which ought specially to appeal to the younger generation because it comes along the very line in which their thought has been trained - the line of scientific enquiry. Another point of interest about the observations of the Theosophical students is that they give, I think, somewhat greater detail than the scriptures, and they arrange their facts in tabular form so that the relation between them can be clearly seen.

If I were asked to teach anyone what I know about the astral plane, I think the first thing that I should tell him is that he should get into his mind the utter reality of it. That should be less difficult for an Indian than for a Western audience. Try to realize that this other condition of existence is just as real (*or just as unreal*) as this. There are philosophers who would say that all existence is illusion - that we ourselves are unreal - that I am deluded when I think I am speaking, and that you are hallucinated when you think you are listening; but however that may be, while we live on this physical plane we have to act as though we were real, and the same thing exactly applies to the astral plane. If this physical world be nothing but an utter delusion, then the same may be true of the astral; but if there be any measure of reality connected with this world in which we are now living, just the same measure of reality belongs to the astral plane also. Remember, I do not mean that either of them is permanent. If you ask whether the physical plane is permanent, I should say "No; the matter of which it is composed is permanent, but not necessarily in this form." All physical matter may become astral matter, all astral matter may become mental matter, and perhaps that is the way in which the Supreme withdraws into Himself. When the scientist is able to examine the atom of the physical plane as it has been examined clairvoyantly, he will find that it is nothing but a vortex center, held in its spiral shape simply by the force flowing through it, just as you may see at the street corner a little whirling column of dust and leaves held in position by the wind circulating through it. The very atom which is at the back of all physical matter is nothing but an ordered aggregation of astral atoms; and if it should please the Logos of our system to withdraw His power, the whole physical world would fall at once into what would be, for us, non-manifestation. That shows you the relation of the astral plane to the physical; it is just as much a material plane - simply another condition of the same matter.

Furthermore, I have constantly to explain in Europe and America that this astral plane is not a place; it is not a heaven far away among the stars, but a condition of matter existing here and now, though unperceived. Astral matter surrounds us at the moment, just as physical matter surrounds us. You are all acquainted with the scientific theory that ether interpenetrates every substance, even the hardest diamond. Just in the same way as ether interpenetrates ordinary physical matter, so does astral matter in its turn interpenetrate ether. Scientists used to think of the ether as a homogeneous substance; now they appear to admit that it is not so, since they say that everything is constructed of electrons. The truth is that ether is itself atomic, and its atoms do not touch one another, but are floating in a sea of still finer matter, which we call astral. But astral matter in its turn may be reduced until we come to the astral atom; that in its turn is found to be floating in a sea of finer matter still. Now these are not different kinds of matter, but different conditions of the same matter. Some of your magicians have been able to make a physical object disappear from its place and re-appear somewhere else. That is in reality a very simple feat of dematerialization. We may make a block of ice invisible by melting it and then boiling the resulting water; in the form of steam it may be forced through a grating or any porous substance, and, on the other side, if subjected to a sufficiently low temperature, it may again be condensed into an exactly similar block of ice. If this could be done rapidly enough the transfer of the block of ice from one chamber to another would seem miraculous; and this is a precise analogy to what takes place in the case of dematerialization. The magician by an effort of his trained will simply reduces the object to a state of matter in which it is invisible to our senses, but it is none the less material for that - just as the steam is matter as surely as the ice. If it is to be called real in one condition it must be called real in the other; if it is to be called unreal in one of these conditions it must also be called unreal in the other.

What is Reality?

Some of you may find it helpful if you recollect that things are real or unreal to us according to the place in which our consciousness is focused. While our consciousness is focused in the physical brain, physical matter alone is perceptible to us, and so it alone seems real, and although we are living in the midst of the astral world at this moment, to most of us it is unreal because it is imperceptible. A few hours later we shall fall asleep, and our consciousness will change its focus from the physical body to the astral body. Then it will be from astral objects alone that we shall be able to receive vibrations, and so those will seem perceptible and real, and the physical objects, though of course they still surround us as before, will be invisible and will therefore seem unreal. But it is not the condition of things which has changed, it is simply the focus of our consciousness. These physical objects are after all manifestations of the Logos on this plane, and they remain manifestations even when we no longer see them. We are not justified, therefore, in saying that all these things are unreal because it is possible for us to raise our consciousness to a higher level. In that case it is our consciousness that has been modified, not His manifestation.

The Results of Vibration

If we take up a modern book on physics, we shall find that it usually gives us a table of octaves of vibration, and we cannot but be struck by the fact that only a very small proportion of them appeal to our senses at all. Since all the information that we possess with regard to the outer world has reached us by means of the very few vibrations to which we are normally able to respond, it is abundantly obvious that the clairvoyant who learns to be sensitive to the whole of this part of the gamut will gain a vast amount of additional knowledge about the world in which he lives.

We shall notice that the slower rates of vibration (*such as sound-waves*) affect the comparatively coarse conditions of matter, and set the air in motion; while the more rapid rates (*such as light*) do not affect the air at all, but act upon finer conditions, such as ether. So that when we have realized the existence of astral matter, which is still subtler than the ether, we shall be prepared to find that the forces playing through it are still higher rates of vibration which do not normally affect any physical matter. Investigation shows us that among these higher vibrations are those caused by the desires and emotions of man, and such of his thoughts as are mingled with personal craving or feeling. It is found that such thoughts or emotions are outpourings of energy just as definite as electricity or steam; but this energy acts at its own level and in its own finer type of matter. That is not a mere supposition, but a definite fact observed over and over again by clairvoyant investigators. All the pictures that are drawn for you in our books, illustrating the effects of affection, of devotion or of avarice, are simply the tabulations of observations made upon astral matter - observations which have been repeated many times with substantially the same results. A whole new world is thus opened before us - a world of finer matter pressing upon us on every side; and to this finer type of matter the name "astral" was given by the mediaeval alchemists.

Since this matter surrounds us all the time, in what way is it acting upon us and in what way are we acting upon it? Once more investigate, and you will find that it is constantly reacting upon us, and that we can no more ignore our astral than our physical surroundings. As the world is at present constituted, physical surroundings are by no means unimportant, and we must learn something of the physical world and its forces if we wish to be able to utilize them to help others, or to resist their undue influence upon ourselves. In exactly the same way, if we wish to be able to protect ourselves from undesirable influences from the astral world, and to have its forces at our command for altruistic work, we must study its conditions and its possibilities; for in this case as in every other, knowledge is power.

The Extension of Knowledge

We find that the laws which govern it are the same with which we are familiar in connection with physical matter - the laws of cause and effect, of action and reaction, and of the conservation of energy; and this fact brings the planes into relation, and shows us that we have to deal not with some strange new world but with another and subtler portion of the old one. The truth is that in studying the astral plane we are simply extending our knowledge of nature a little further in a direction in which it has already been extended more than once. Primitive man, knowing nothing but what was obvious to his senses, can have been aware only of the solid and liquid forms of matter; to him the tempest must have been an inexplicable manifestation of an awful invisible force, and the death which followed the inhalation of noxious fumes must have seemed the mysterious visitation of the deity. Think how great must have been the extension of knowledge and comprehension of nature when from careful observations a theory of gases was deduced, and gradually won its way into universal acceptation! An entirely new realm had opened before those primitive physicists when they thus learnt to study and experiment with this finer condition of matter. A long step further in the same direction was taken when the existence of ether was realized, for by that knowledge many phenomena became explicable which before were deemed miraculous. In earlier days natural laws were but little understood and the world was supposed to be governed by divine caprice; but with each advance of science the domain of law and order was extended, and the unknown outer void in which miracles might happen was decreased. When we suggest the study of the astral plane we are simply recommending another step, but always along the same line of experimenting with ever subtler forms of matter and when this step is taken it will be found that the action of man's thoughts and emotions has been brought within range of law.

Theosophy is Advanced Science

In this sense it may accurately be said that the students of Theosophy are the advanced scientists of the day, for they are engaged in examining a field just a little ahead of that which has approved itself to the majority of physicists. Do not forget that our great founder, Madame Blavatsky, displayed a very remarkable knowledge of science, though she does not seem to have learnt it along ordinary lines. She made certain statements in connection with it which were ridiculed at the time, yet the facts which she announced have since been accepted and approved by the most competent authorities. An account of these has been given by Mrs. Besant in "Theosophy and Science", the fourth lecture in "Theosophy applied to Human Life", and Theosophists should familiarize themselves with it. Obviously if one who had not taken up the study of ordinary physical science is yet found to know more of it than its foremost professors knew at the time when she wrote it, it is well worth while to examine what she has said with regard to fields as yet untouched by them.

Science has attained its marvelous results by means of highly perfected instruments; such results as have been attained by the pupils of Madame Blavatsky have been gained in an entirely different way - the way recommended by your teachers of old - the development not of the instrument but of the observer. It is by the employment of that method that Theosophical writers have been able to give you some details of the arrangement of the higher planes and the conditions of life upon them.

I have intentionally avoided the repetition in this lecture of the information as to these conditions which anyone who wishes may find in the manual called "The Astral Plane"; instead I have tried to take up the subject with you in its more general aspect in relation to this lower plane, so that you may appreciate the astral as just as much a part of the great world in which we live as is the physical, and may realize that if we want to live wisely and to the best advantage we must endeavor to understand the whole of our world, and not only the lowest part of it.

How it Affects Us

This astral world affects us because its vibrations have the same qualities as all other kinds of vibrations - they radiate in all directions, and they tend to reproduce themselves. If two stringed instruments are tuned accurately together, and placed near to one another, it is found that when a note is struck upon one of them, the other vibrates in unison. The vibration of the note radiates in all directions, but when it falls upon something capable of exact response it at once reproduces itself.

If by emotion or passion you set up a vibration in astral matter, it acts in precisely the same way; and necessarily in its radiation it impinges upon the astral bodies of all those about you. If there be among them one which is in tune with that vibration, it will at once be excited to respond to it; that is to say, your emotion will be reproduced in that other man. If, however, that astral body is already pulsating strongly at some different rate, your vibration will not find it in tune, and so cannot affect it. Suppose a man is under the influence of anger, and you are full of gentleness and affection. His astral body is vibrating vigorously at a certain rate; he is in such a condition of palpitation that he does not even feel your gentle radiations; he goes on along his own line, quite uninfluenced by it, just as the man under the sway of wild passion on the physical plane is blind to all suggestions of reason.

The Appearance of the Astral Body

People often ask as to the appearance of these astral bodies, and those who have seen one occasionally are sometimes surprised to find that it does not resemble the pictures given in some of our books, such as "Man, Visible and Invisible." They forget that that book was written specially to draw attention to the colors in the luminous ovoid of astral matter, and the effect upon those colors of different emotions and passions, so that a vivid illustration might be given of the way in which man's evolution is affected by the thoughts and feelings of every-day life. Therefore those bodies were drawn, as it were, out of proportion, one part of them being specially emphasized, and another part studiously kept in the background. You may remember that the physical form is outlined in pencil only, in order to show the relative size of the ovoid. In reality that counterpart of the physical body is far more prominent than it is shown in those drawings. It is an exact duplicate of the physical form, perfectly distinct from the surrounding luminous matter, and therefore perfectly recognizable. Every type of physical matter has its corresponding type in astral matter, and the latter is very strongly attracted by the former. There is a counterpart in astral matter for every physical object, and that counterpart is always of suitable type. So that wherever there is solid physical matter it is interpenetrated by astral matter of the lowest sub-plane; where there is physical liquid matter it is interpenetrated by astral matter of the second sub-plane from the bottom; and whether there is physical gas it is interpenetrated by astral matter of the third sub-plane from the bottom, and so on. Just as there is no difficulty in distinguishing a solid object from the air surrounding it on the physical plane, so is there no difficulty in distinguishing its astral counterpart from what we may call the astral air, which surrounds it.

While it is true that a man's astral body takes that ovoid shape which is the visible manifestation, on these lower planes, of the shape of the causal body, it is also true that of the mass of matter contained within that ovoid perhaps ninety-nine per cent is contained within the periphery of the physical form. The reason of this is the very strong attraction exercised by that physical form over the astral matter, and the further fact that when a kind of habit of remaining in a particular form - a sort of momentum of circulation of the astral currents - has been set up, that habit or that momentum will persist for a long time after the cause of it has been withdrawn. Thus although during sleep one leaves his physical body on the bed and moves about in his astral vehicle, the latter continues to retain the exact appearance of the former; and even when the physical body is finally laid aside at death the habit still persists, and the form is still retained through any ordinary length of astral life.

With regard to this matter of appearance there is another point to be borne in mind, and that is that astral matter is far more plastic than physical, and is readily molded by the action of thought. If a man thinks of himself as having a particular form the matter of his astral body will for the moment be molded into that form, and will retain it as long as his thought is firmly fixed upon it; but the moment that he forgets, or his attention is distracted, the astral matter will come under the sway of its habit, and will at once flow back into its natural shape. So that a man can take on any appearance that he pleases, but cannot retain it permanently without devoting the whole of his time to that one thought. Nevertheless a thought, which is almost constantly present in his mind does slowly effect a permanent change. That is true to some extent upon the physical plane; the man who for years leads a debased life presently begins to show signs of it in face and form, while the man who has turned from an evil life to one of purity and holiness presently shows a very decided improvement in physical appearance. Although such a change usually takes places gradually, instances are not wanting in which it has been startlingly rapid. Some cases of what is called "Mind-cure" illustrate this, as does also the appearance of the stigmata upon the bodies of various ecstatics. Madame Blavatsky gives some very remarkable cases of this in "Isis Unveiled". Since astral matter is so much more readily affected than physical, it is comprehensible that a similar change should occur more rapidly in the case of this astral vehicle.

Suffering After Death

All religions tell us that the conditions of existence after death depend very largely upon the kind of life which the man has led upon the physical plane; that if his life has been good and pure he will find himself happy, but if his earthly course has been gross and evil, trouble and suffering may ensue from it. Unfortunately in some forms of Christian teaching these joys have been regarded as reward and this suffering as punishment; and much grievous misunderstanding has resulted from this clumsy mistake. If in physical life a man seizes hold of a red-hot iron bar his hand will be burnt; but it will hardly occur to him to say that God has punished him for taking hold of that bar. He will say rather that what has happened is the natural result of his own action, and anybody who understands anything of science can explain to him exactly the mechanism of the occurrence, and show him how the intensely rapid vibrations of the hot iron bar have torn apart the tissues of his hand, and so produced what we call a burn. We shall never understand the conditions of life after death until we realize that happiness follows upon good thought or action and suffering upon evil thought or action, in exactly the same way as the burn follows the contact with the hot iron. The cause and its effect are related as the two sides of a coin are related; and just as we cannot draw towards us the obverse side of the coin without also drawing towards us its reverse, so we cannot commit any action or give birth to any thought without at the same time bringing ourselves its result as a definite part of the original action.

The more ignorant among the Christians often speak of the providence of God, and in using that term they mean to imply that the Supreme Being is constantly personally interfering with the working of His own laws, and they usually also imply that He can be induced at their request to exercise such power of interference. This theory also involves the idea that He has originally planned His universe so badly that the machinery needs this constant tinkering in order to make it work satisfactorily - surely not an exalted conception of the Deity. Nothing could be further from the glorious truth, for one of the most striking characteristics of even that small part of the Divine world which we are able to see is its marvelous adaptability and the wonderful elasticity of its action. Men often find it difficult to recognize the accurate working of the law of justice in their own case, even though they cannot but admit that in all the realms of nature there can never be an effect without its appropriate cause.

Common though this position is, we may see its absurdity by taking a very simple analogy. The man who is using an engine expects to get out of it an amount of work proportionate to the amount of energy put into it, say in the form of fuel. He allows for a certain waste from friction, and for a certain amount given off in the form of heat, but still there is a definite proportion of work which he expects to get out of his engine, because he knows that there is a natural law of the conservation of energy. Suppose he should find that he is not getting a proper proportion of work from that engine, we should esteem him a very foolish man if he therefore declared that the law of the conservation of energy was all a delusion and a mistake. If we could suppose him to be so ignorant as to say that his experiment with his machine tended to show that there was no such thing, we should reply that there had been other experiments besides his, and that the law was already established as a definite certainty. It would never occur to the intelligent engineer to doubt for a moment the universal application of that law; he would at once turn to his machine and examine that in order to find the defect which caused the loss of energy. Yet the very same man who is so certain of the inviolability of Nature's law in one direction will begin to grumble about injustice if any suffering or sorrow comes to him; whereas the analogy of his own line of thought with regard to the machine would show that the only sensible conclusion would be that since the law of justice is perfect in its working there must undoubtedly have been something wrong in his own action in the past to account for this sorrow which has fallen upon him.

The Advantage of the Study

Unquestionably the study of astral and mental forces and of the astral and mental worlds generally helps us to understand how this mighty law of justice produces its results. That is one reason why I think the study of these higher portions of nature so useful to us. It supplements our knowledge of the physical world, and enables us to form a far more complete conception of the whole great scheme, and it is obvious that this wider knowledge must make us of greater use. We see constantly in every-day life that good intentions without knowledge are not sufficient to produce a satisfactory result, for we frequently find that the well-meaning man blunders terribly, and often does more harm than good. Indeed a cynical philosopher has remarked that more harm is done in the world by the ignorant but well-meaning man than by the really wicked. If we do not wish to swell the ranks of the ignorant but well-meaning, we must set ourselves definitely to the acquisition of knowledge - knowledge which shall include the higher planes as well as the lower.

None can doubt that great forces of nature are playing in these realms of finer matter; and if any of them can be used by the unselfish man for the helping of his brother, then I say let us learn all that we can about these forces, whether they be mental, astral or physical. We know that knowledge enables us to give help to our fellows upon the physical plane, and we can see by analogy that if we are to be of use on the astral plane during sleep and after death, we certainly require knowledge there also. Let us then strive to gain such knowledge, and to gain it as soon and as fully as possible, so that no time may be wasted.

I do not for a moment seek to deny or to minimize the possible dangers of the astral plane. A man may misuse power upon any plane, and a man may be deceived upon any plane, and therefore on all planes alike he must be on his guard. In "The Voice of the Silence" we read, "Look not for thy Guru in these mâyâvic regions", and the caution is as urgently needed in these days as it could possibly have been in the days of Aryasangha. In Western countries at least there are hundreds of people who have accepted dead men as their teachers, each regarding the particular entity that communicates as a kind of private archangel specially sent by God to teach him or her. The Indian student ought not to need to be warned against such a mistake as this.

In the same book we are told that we must find our teacher on the mental plane - that his instruction must appeal to us through our intellect and not merely through our emotions. You may remember that one of your great Indian teachers, Siddhartha Gautama, whom men call the Buddha, especially cautioned his followers not to accept teaching which came to them by presumed spiritual inspiration, as from a deva - that is to say, not to accept it merely because it came in that way, but to judge it as all kinds of teaching must be judged - by the standard of one's own reason and one's own common sense. It is quite obvious that the dead man is not omniscient just because he happens to be dead; it is true that he has certain additional opportunities, but it by no means follows that he knows how to make use of them, and we must receive any statements that he makes with precisely the same reservations as we should have received statements made by him before he died.

If we adopt that method of testing everything by reason and by common sense we shall be quite safe in our efforts to understand the astral world. Remember that in that same book, "The Voice of the Silence", this astral world is spoken of as the 'Hall of Learning', showing that there is much valuable information to be acquired there by the student who approaches it wisely. If we thus keep the mind steady and the understanding clear, and if we test everything carefully as it comes to us, we shall never be drawn aside from the pursuit of the goal that lies before us by any temptation which the astral plane can offer. For those of us who are beginning to realize the existence and nature of the great divine scheme of evolution, the privilege of trying in our small way to help it forward is the one purpose of our existence. Of course it is true that that great scheme will be fulfilled whether we add to it our tiny mite of effort or not, yet it is unquestionably part of that scheme that those who have learned to understand it should co-operate intelligently in it, and that such effort is expected from us, and that its fulfillment will be hastened if we learn to throw our energies into it. We know that there will be those who will help; why should we not be among them? To us as to all is offered the opportunity of working as instruments in the hand of God; why should we not accept this opportunity? Since that glorious karma must come to some among men, let it be to us; why should we not be among those who share it? And yet, if we have really seen the glory of that scheme, it will be without any thought of karma that may accrue to us that we shall throw our whole hearts into the work; it will be simply because, having seen the grandeur and the beauty of the plan, there can be for us no other possibility than to devote the whole of our energies to trying to forward it. Let us then study any portion of that scheme which comes in our way, whether it be spiritual or mental, astral or physical, for all alike are parts of this great divine plan. Let us never for a moment lose sight of the goal which lies before us and of the spiritual development which is necessary for the attainment of that goal. But as long as we live in these lower planes, let us live well; and we can live well only if we live intelligently, and we can live intelligently only if we study the great laws of this universe of which we are a part.

THE ATTITUDE OF THE ENQUIRER

I have received many letters from those who are put in the position of lecturers and teachers of Theosophy, asking how best to meet the constant demands of enquirers for proof of the accuracy of the Theosophical teaching. Another common remark of the enquirer is: "You have a large literature; I am a busy man. Where am I to begin in all this? Give me the most important part first." Instead of writing a number of private letters, I have thought it best to put an answer, once for all, in the pages of *The Adyar Bulletin*, to which later enquirers can be referred.

What should be the attitude of the enquirer towards the wonderful mass of new truth, which is put before him in Theosophical teaching? It should be an intelligently receptive attitude — not one of carping criticism on the one hand, nor of blind belief on the other, but of endeavor to understand the different facts as they are presented to him, and to make them his own. In Theosophy we strongly deprecate the attitude of blind belief, for we say that it has been the cause of a vast amount of the evil of the world. On this point the teaching of the Eastern Masters is emphatic, for they regard superstition as one of the fetters which it is absolutely necessary that a man should cast off before he can hope to make any progress on the occult Path. They also regard doubt as a fetter, but they say that the only way to get rid of doubt is not by blind faith, but by the acquisition of knowledge. It would be quite useless for a man to exchange blind faith in orthodox Christianity for a similar blind faith in those who happened to be writing or speaking on Theosophy. To say: "Thus saith Madame Blavatsky or Mrs. Besant," is after all only a small advance on saying: "Thus saith St. Paul or St. John."

We who live in western countries have a bad heredity behind us in these matters, for the point of view of our forefathers has usually been either the blind faith of the unintelligent and biased person, or the blank and rather militant incredulity of the materialist. We have been too much in the habit of thinking that what does not happen in Europe or America is not worth taking account of, and that nobody outside of ourselves knows anything at all. Many of us have grown up in the midst of the ridiculous theory that there was only one religion in the world, and that the vast majority of its inhabitants were *heathens*, whom we had to save and that if we could not do that, they must be left to *the uncovenanted mercies of God*. It seems incredible that civilized people could ever believe anything so silly, but what I state is actually the fact. When we think that we may have had among our recent ancestors people who were capable of that, we see at once that we are but ill-prepared for the reception of a rational creed.

Again, we have been unfortunate in that we had not even the whole of Christianity, for history shows us that what has been taught to us is only a dismembered fragment of the original form of that religion. Before the Gnostic doctors were cast out, Christianity had a system of philosophy fully equal to that of the other religions, but after their departure it was but a truncated faith. Still its ethics remained to it, and they will be found to be exactly the same as those of the other great world-faiths. In Theosophy we hold that it matters little what a man believes, but much what he does; whether he is kind and noble, just and gentle, pure and true.

It may be of interest to western readers to remember that on this subject the teaching of the Christian scripture is exactly the same as that of Theosophy. In the twenty-fifth chapter of Matthew will be found a striking account, said to have been given by the Christ Himself, of what is commonly called the day of judgment, when all men are to be brought before Him and their final destiny is to be decided according to the answer which they are able to give to His questions. Remember that, according to the theory, the Christ Himself is to be the judge on that occasion, and therefore He can make no mistake as to the procedure. What then are the questions upon the answers to which the future of these men is to depend? From what one hears of modern Christianity one would expect that the first question would be: "Do you believe in Me?" and the second one: "Do you attend Church regularly?" The Christ, however, unaccountably forgets to ask either of these questions. He asks: "Did you feed the hungry, did you give drink to the thirsty, did you clothe the naked, did you visit those who were sick and in prison? That is to say, were you ordinarily kind and charitable in your relations to your fellow-men?"

And it is according to the answers to *those* questions that the destiny of the man is decided. So far as He, the Judge, has explained Himself, any heathen who had done these things would at once pass into eternal felicity, for He says no single word about belief at all. As regards all these virtues the teachings of all the religions are identical. The daily life of a really good Christian will be found to be identical with that of a really good Buddhist or a really good Hindu. One will call his religious exercises by the name of prayer, while the others call them meditation, but in the nature of them there is little difference. Each enjoins the practice of the same virtues; each reprobates the same vices.

We must clear our minds utterly of the extraordinary theory that a man's religion is a question of importance. It depends entirely upon where the man happens to be born. You are, let us say, a Christian, and you cannot conceive it as possible that you could have been anything else; yet if you had been born in an Indian family, you would have belonged just as unquestioningly to the Hindu religion, or to the Buddhist if you had been born in Ceylon or Siam. Therefore we must entirely cast aside the curious prejudice that it is necessary for a man to hold some particular form of religion if he is to obtain final perfection.

On taking up the study of Theosophy it is necessary that we should adopt an entirely new attitude — that we should open the doors of the mind, and learn to treat religion as a matter of common-sense, exactly as we do science. On the one hand we must accept nothing, which does not commend itself to us as reasonable, and on the other hand we must not expect proofs of a nature incongruous with the fact, which we are considering. It is often impossible to give for psychological problems and theories a demonstration along mathematical lines, or a proof on the physical plane, which a man can hold in his hand. The proof of any proposition must be congruous with the nature of the proposition, and consequently the final proof of some of the deepest Theosophical doctrines must lie in the experience of the evolved soul.

A common-sense attitude will enable us to determine whether we can know a certain thing positively, or whether it is necessary to take first what seems to be a reasonable working hypothesis, and then see how far future experience supports or weakens it. Much of the Theosophical teaching must remain as a hypothesis for each man until he is able to develop powers by which he can see for himself; but in the meantime he may easily acquire *practical* certainty with regard to it, by weighing it against all other hypotheses and seeing how perfectly it, and it alone, accounts for the observed phenomena of life. This is exactly the ground on which are held a large number of what are commonly called scientific facts.

It is a valuable exercise for the student to think carefully which of his beliefs in ordinary life are really founded upon direct personal knowledge. He believes, for example, that the earth rotates upon its axis; yet all the evidence of his daily life goes to prove exactly the contrary. The ground is stable beneath his feet, and he cannot in any way prove to himself that the sun, moon and stars do not really move above him, exactly as they appear to do. There *is* proof available of the rotation of the earth. There is the Foucault pendulum experiment and the experiment with the gyroscope. If a man has seen those experiments tried, he *knows* that the earth rotates; if he has not, he does not know it, but only believes it. He believes it on good evidence, but it is not the evidence of his senses. A reasonable hypothesis is necessary in order to induce a man to work, and here his imagination comes into play. He must be evolved enough to imagine a thing as possible, or he must be able to abstract his ideas and deduce from them a working principle, before he can be induced to make an effort towards proving a fact as true.

Theosophy presents to the student several working hypotheses, which appeal to his reason, and at the same time it promises him success in demonstrating them to be true, if he will do certain things. It tells him that some men have already had success in this demonstration, that they have been able to develop in themselves certain powers which enable them to know that these things are true, and that therefore it is possible for him also to do this, though it does not conceal from him the difficulty of the undertaking.

Theosophy has a considerable literature, but it has no inspired Scriptures. We who write books on the various branches of the subject, put before our friends the results of our investigations, and we take every care that what we state shall be scrupulously accurate as far as our knowledge goes but the model which we set before us when we write is not the sacred Scripture but the scientific manual. So far as the western world is concerned, the study of Theosophical subjects is comparatively a new one, although in the East many books have been written in which these matters are expounded; but these oriental books naturally do not approach them from the modern scientific point of view. Our plan in verifying the information originally given to us has been just what was adopted in the beginning of the sciences of chemistry or astronomy — a careful observation of all the phenomena within reach, their tabulation, and the endeavor to deduce from them the general laws which govern them.

We are then in the position of the early students of a new science, and although, thanks to the information we have received from eastern Teachers, we have already grasped the main outline of our science, our own investigations are constantly adding to our knowledge of its detail, and this fact often makes it necessary for us to modify statements made in the earlier days of the movement, and to amend imperfect or premature generalizations. The details will increase in number and accuracy as the number of those who can make the investigations increases, but the broad outlines of principles, which have been given to us will always remain the same.

Our attitude to Theosophy should, I think, be thus characterized:

(1) We must not exchange the blind belief in the authority of the Church for an equally blind faith in personal Theosophical teachers.

(2) We must preserve an open mind and an intelligently receptive attitude.

(3) We should accept as working hypotheses the truths, which are given to us, and should set to work to prove them for ourselves.

(4) We should realize that this teaching sets before us the scheme of the Logos for His universe, and that the condition of making progress in that universe is to learn the rules of that scheme, and set ourselves to work with them and not against them.

(5) We should seek development or progress not for the sake of ourselves, but in order that the knowledge we may acquire may be used for the benefit of humanity, and that we may fit ourselves to be the servants of that humanity.

(6) We must change absolutely our point of view towards life. When regarding the sorrow and suffering of the world, we must put aside the despairing attitude of the theologian for one of hopefulness, because the teaching fills us with the calm certainty that everything will at last be well.

The Relative Importance of the Truths

Again, Theosophy lays before us a vast mass of new truths with regard to the constitution both of man and of the universe, and also with regard to their past and future. Though the outline is simple the detail is considerable. We have therefore to think in what order we shall consider these truths; what is their relative importance. It seems to me that they group themselves naturally into three great classes: first, the ethical teachings, and the reason for them; second, the explanation of the constitution of man and the planes on which he lives; third, the remainder of the teaching, the great mass of information about planetary chains and earlier races of mankind.

They come thus in order of importance, because the knowledge of the ethical teaching and the reason for it is necessary for the daily life of man, because as he learns even a little of it he can instantly proceed to put it into practice. If, having learnt so much, something should occur to prevent him from learning more, he will still have gained a priceless possession — one, which will affect the whole of his future life, not in this world only but in others also.

The second block of information, with regard to the constitution of man and the world in which he lives, is also of great importance to him, as showing him how to do many of the things which the first division of the teaching has commended to him, as showing him also how to be much more useful to his fellow-men than he could be without this knowledge.

The third block of teaching, though keenly interesting, is less directly practical. It has its value; it has a great value; for from the past we may in many cases predict the future, and from it we may learn many a lesson, which will be of help to us in that future. At the same time one must admit that a man might be just as loyal a subject, just as good a citizen, and just as useful to his fellow-men if he had never heard about the planetary chains; whereas it is not true that he would be just as good in any of those capacities if he remained ignorant of the first and second of our great classes of truths.

First, the ethics and the reason for them. The ethical teaching of Theosophy is precisely the same as that of any and all of the great religions. There is therefore nothing new for us to learn here; the only difference is that Theosophy gives us a scientific reason for our ethics, which most religions do not. This consideration of the reason for ethical teaching involves a very large block of the Theosophical teaching, for the ultimate reason for all good action is that it may be in harmony with the divine plan, the will of the Logos. That we may understand what will be in harmony with it, we must first try to grasp as much as is possible for us of that divine plan itself. This involves the consideration of the nature of God and the method of His working, and also His relation to man. Under this head we mast 'speak of the Logos of our solar system, and the beginnings of that system, of the atom and planes, of the nature, of the formation, constitution and development of man, and of the methods appointed for that development, and the way in which he can hasten it, and of the obstacles which he will find in his way.

Under the second heading we must take up in greater detail the various vehicles of man and their relation to the different planes of nature. We must learn to understand ourselves, in order that we may direct intelligently the complicated machinery of the vehicles. This is an intensely practical consideration for us; we are living upon all these planes now, though most of us do not know it; we are using our mental and astral bodies as bridges to carry to the physical brain the messages from the ego, and to carry back to him in return the information which they obtain from external impacts of all sorts. Unless we understand these bodies we cannot use them to the best advantage, we cannot get out of them all that we might. Apart from the fact of that constant use of the vehicles, we all spend about a third of our lives in the astral body — in a state which we commonly call sleep. After physical death we enter upon a long life in these higher vehicles, and it becomes once more obvious that the more we know about them the more efficient and the more comfortable will this life be. These higher bodies have their powers and their capacities as well as the physical body. If we understand them we can utilize all these for our own advancement and for the helping of our fellows, so that their study is eminently practical.

The third division is that which treats of the past evolution of man. It deals with the planetary chain of which our earth is a part, with its relation to other chains in the solar system, and with the successive life-waves, which have passed over these chains. It takes up the question of the work of the great Official who superintends the formation of each Root Race and its subdivision into branch races. It explains how men come to be at such different levels in life, and accounts for the formation of classes and castes. Although this appears to be less practical than the other kinds, we shall find not only that it is intensely interesting, but that it has its uses as well. It is a remarkable fact that all religions have made it a special point to teach their followers something of the beginnings of the world and of man. In the Jewish scripture you have the extraordinary story of the earlier chapters of the *Book of Genesis*, which is unfortunately adopted just as it stands by the Christian Church; but each religion has some such story — even those of savage tribes. It is clear therefore that those who found religions must know that this information is of great importance for man. Madame Blavatsky has followed in the footsteps of her Teachers in that respect, for the whole of her monumental work, *The Secret Doctrine*, is a sermon upon the text of the *Stanzas of Dzyan*, which give an account of the origin of man and of our system.

The point of first importance is that we should live the life; the second that we should understand our possibilities; and when we have got so far, we may then take up with advantage the study of past history. In following out thoroughly that first block of teaching, we have arrived at certainty in regard to the rest. "If any man will do His will, he shall know of the doctrine." The best way to prove to oneself the truth of these Theosophical doctrines is to take them for granted and to live as though they were true; then the proof will soon come.

WHY NOT I?

Men join the Theosophical Society for various reasons; some because they sympathize with its objects, some because they think they can learn something from it, some because they meant to help the work it is doing. Whatever be their reasons, when they have grasped the principle of evolution, they are usual fired with enthusiasm for it. Seeing the possibility and the desirability of progress, they begin to be anxious to attain it; hearing how sadly the world needs helping, they wish to enroll themselves in the noble army of martyrs who devote themselves to that stupendous but somewhat thankless task — thankless, because the world still stones its prophets, and the discomfort of the process is but little mitigated by the prospect that a wiser posterity will presently raise monuments to them. When members have thus decided to hasten the process of their evolution, they enquire as to methods, teachers, helpers, and they soon hear from older students of the existence of the Brotherhood of Adepts, and of the fact that some of these Great Ones occasionally admit apprentices and instruct them in the work which has to be done. The aspirant feels that this is exactly what he would like, and he wishes to offer himself at once for such a position. But the older student explains to him that the offer must come from the other side — that all he can do is to make himself fit for such a post, and wait until the Master calls him.

When he further enquires as to the way in which he can make himself fit to be chosen, he is told that there is no mystery as to the qualifications required. They have been elaborately described in the sacred books of the ancients, they may be found in the teaching of every religion, and they are worked out minutely in modern Theosophical literature. It is easy to learn about them, but difficult to acquire them, and their practice seems out of touch with much that we find prominent in the life of the present day. History assures us that the thing has been done, but closer examination shows us that it has never been done exactly under existing conditions. Whenever in older times a man set himself definitely to live the higher life, he began by retiring to a cave or a habitation far removed from the world of men. So long as he remained among his fellows he was supposed to be living the life of the householder, who might be, and ought to be, a thoroughly good and honest man, but was engaged in doing the work of the world on the physical plane and not aiming specially at occult development. He participated in that higher life by making it possible for others, by providing for the needs of those who were wholly devoting themselves to it.

Now the hermit who lives in a cave or the monk who confines himself to his cell no doubt resigns what are commonly called the pleasures of the world, but he provides himself with admirably appropriate conditions for the work which he is trying to do. He sees very little of his fellow-creatures; he has cast aside all responsibilities; he has nothing to worry or trouble him, nothing to make him angry. Such a life is possible only for men of a certain temperament; but for them it is ideal in its freedom. That, however, is not at all the method of development recommended to the Theosophical student; he is expected to acquire the qualifications while still mixing with his fellows and trying to help them. Usually he has his living to get; he is constantly meeting other men, who are sometimes pleasant and sometimes the reverse, but in any case bring with them their own vibrations, which are different from his own, and so disturbing. He has his anxieties, he 'has inevitably many things about which he must think, and under those conditions he cannot expect to make such rapid progress in occult development as a man who has nothing else to do. At the same time, he can in certain ways do more good than a hermit. He can set an example; he can show by his life that it is possible to be in the world and yet not of the world.

One who desires to be accepted and taught by a Master should endeavor to understand exactly what the Master wants, and how the matter of receiving a man as an apprentice must envisage itself to Him. Every human being has a certain amount of spiritual strength, just as he has a certain amount of physical strength. Most men are ignorant of its very existence, and so let it lie dormant or fritter it away. A Master knows exactly how much force He has, and holds it to be His duty to use every ounce of it to the best advantage for the good of the world. It is that consideration, and that only, which determines whether He will or will not accept any person as an apprentice. There is no sort of favoritism about it. He does not take a person because he is recommended, or because he is the son of somebody who has been accepted before. Sometimes a student thinks:

"I know I am defective, but still I should like to be taught and helped; why should not the Master accept and teach us all?"

That is unreasonable, because to do that would not be a profitable investment of the Master's force. Any older student can teach a newcomer, and to ask the Master to do it would be like asking the Principal of a College or the Minister of Education of a country to teach an infant class. The Master is dealing with men en masse, in great blocks of thousands at a time, and in quite a different way; and we have to consider what is best for all, not for ourselves alone. It would be obviously unwise for the man who is Director of Education for a whole country to devote his time to teaching one little child, or even twenty or thirty. If the Master sees a promising person, we may imagine Him making a calculation in His mind. We may with all reverence suppose that He would say to Himself:

"If I accept that man, I shall have to spend so many hours over him; during that time I could do a certain amount of the wider work for the world. But I think that when he has been brought to a certain point he will be able to do work which will in the long run more than counterbalance what I could do in the time spent over him, and meantime he can be used as a channel; therefore he is a good investment."

Acceptance depends solely upon the fitness of the candidate. It is by no means only a question of what he will be able to do some day in the future, but also of how far he can be used here and now. Take an example. In the course of His work a Master may wish to produce some physical result — to send out an etheric current perhaps — in a certain town. He is working on the spiritual or intuitional level; how can He most easily achieve that physical result?

Several methods are available. He can project His force to the required spot at the spiritual level, and then drive it down by main force through the intervening planes; but that will waste a great deal of energy in the process of distribution. He can call to some pupil at a distance, give him the force on the higher plane, and tell him to go astrally to the spot where it is needed, and then transfer it to the physical level. That would take less of the Master's energy, but would expend more than is necessary of the pupil's. But suppose the Master had in that town a good student who had brought himself into harmony with the great work. He would utilize that man; He would pour the energy into him at the higher level, and use him as a channel for it, leaving to him the transmutation into physical-plane energy and the actual radiation of it in this lower world. The student as an ego would be conscious of the honor done to him, and would eagerly co-operate; but the personality in its physical brain might not know what was being done, though it would be sure to feel much uplifted and unexpectedly happy. When that feeling comes to the student, he may take it for granted that some blessing is being shed through him; when he wakes in the morning with a sensation of bliss and great content, he may know thereby that some good thing has been done through him.

It will be readily understood that a man who can often be used in that way is one whom the Master notices and is likely to draw nearer to Himself. Unfortunately men often allow themselves to get into a condition which makes them useless to the Master; then when He wants a channel in their neighborhood, He looks at them and sees that they are not available, and so He chooses someone else to bear that blessing. It may be worth while to consider some of the reasons that make a student temporarily useless to the Master, and to try to understand why certain actions produce that particular result, so that we may avoid them.

First let us grasp the relation of our vehicles to one another. We speak and think of them as separate bodies, each functioning in a different world, and we are apt to forget how entirely they are also one. All matter is fundamentally the same matter; just as all kinds of substances in the physical world are all built of absolutely identical physical atoms, and the only thing that differs is the arrangement of those atoms, so all kinds of matter on the different planes from the highest to the lowest are built of identical bubbles, and the only thing which is different is the arrangement of those bubbles. So there is a very real sense in which it may be said that all our bodies are really one complex body, the different parts of which are closely interrelated.

We may take an analogy from our physical vehicle. As we see it, it is a form of flesh, and has the appearance of being built only of solid matter; but we know quite well that it is thoroughly interpenetrated with liquid, so that the slightest prick in any part of it at once produces a drop of blood. The blood interpenetrates the body so thoroughly that if it were possible (*which it is not*) to remove all the solid matter and yet maintain the liquid in the same position, we should have a perfect outline of the body built up in blood alone. In the same way the body is interpenetrated by air and other gases; and we could conceive, if it were possible in some way instantaneously to freeze those gases, that we might have a perfect outline indicated by them. But all these different kinds of matter make one body, and it would be impossible to affect one of the kinds of matter, which compose it without equally affecting the others also. All the vehicles of which we speak as the causal, mental, astral and physical bodies interpenetrate one another; so that it is impossible to affect one without thereby influencing all the rest.

If therefore a man desires to offer himself as a channel for the force of the Master, he must have all these vehicles simultaneously in a calm and responsive condition; and anything which disturbs such a condition in any one of them will be an obstacle in the way of the Master's work.

One of the commonest of these obstacles is worry. A man who allows himself to feel worried or anxious has his mental body in a condition of unrest, which to clairvoyant vision, gives it the appearance of the ocean when tossed by a tempest. Before a Master could use such a vehicle as a channel for His force, He would have to exert whatever amount of energy was needed to calm that troubled ocean and hold it absolutely still; and that would be far more trouble for Him than to manipulate the force Himself; so He will certainly choose some other way.

Another very common obstacle is selfishness. In a man whose thoughts are centered upon himself, all the forces are moving inward instead of outward. Before such a man could be of any use to the Master, it would be necessary that all those currents should be checked and reversed, that their life-long habit of inward flow should be eradicated, and a new habit of exactly opposite nature should be established. It is at once obvious that to attempt to utilize such a man cannot be a profitable speculation. What the Master wants is a person in whom all the forces are flowing outwards towards others. Then there is already a radiation going on, and when He throws His force in, it is easy for Him to strengthen that radiation. Another point is that, unless the man is absolutely primitive and unevolved, along with the selfishness there is always disturbance. The ego knows something about evolution and the laws which govern it, and therefore his will is always favorable to progress, and so far as he is yet able to guide the personality he guides it in the direction of evolution. When the personality takes the bit between its teeth and runs away, it is always against his will; but the reins by which he holds it are not yet as strong as they will be, and so if he pulls too hard he knows that they will break, which often makes the position very difficult for him. He must make the personality strong in order that effective progress may be possible for it; and yet when it is strong it often uses its strength in directions which he does not approve. Thus wherever there is selfishness there is always at the heart of things a struggle, and that also makes it impossible for the Master to use a self-centered man.

Pride and conceit are forms of selfishness, and they also set the currents running inward instead of outward. A man who is conceited is never upon the watch for opportunities of usefulness, and so he often misses them. He is intent upon going his own way, and he is therefore not open to the influence from the Master, which would set him moving in the opposite direction of helpfulness and service.

Irritability is another bar with which we frequently meet. Just as the mental body of the worried man is in a state of perpetual disturbance, so is the astral body of the irritable man. A healthy astral body should normally exhibit some four or five distinct rates of vibration corresponding to the nobler emotions, and it should show only those vortices which correspond to the principal centers in the physical vehicle; but the irritable man often shows fifty, sixty or a hundred small vortices, each like an open sore in the center of a little tract containing an assortment of all kinds of unpleasant and undesirable colors. Through every one of these the man's force is escaping, and so he wearies himself and wastes strength unnecessarily, scattering round him unhealthy disturbing influences.

A man of this kind has no strength left to be employed in the Master's service; and even if a Master should exert the force necessary to reduce his chaos to order, any streams of energy, which were sent out through him would be tainted by his ill-temper. I know well that for us, who are living in a century of savage hurry, it is difficult to avoid irritability; the haste and pressure of modern life cause great nervous suffering, which is apt to show itself in this very vice of chronic ill-temper. Just because people are overstrained they are often sensitive to things, which in reality do not matter in the least, and should not be allowed to cause disturbance. Under such an influence a man allows himself to be troubled by what another says of him, or by some falsehood which is written about him in a newspaper — things which should not cause even a momentary annoyance to any man of a well-balanced and philosophical turn of mind.

Again, a man who frequently yields himself to depression is quite useless while under its influence. If we turn to the illustration of the astral body of a depressed person in Man, Visible and Invisible, we shall find that he has absolutely enclosed himself in a kind of cage. This cage would prevent the radiation of beneficent influences; and even if they were strong enough to break it, they would still carry parts of it with them, and would be polluted by it. Also, to break up such a cage in that violent manner would break up the astral body itself and cause serious harm. The same thing is true of avarice, though the coloration of the cage is different.

Another difficulty, which sometimes stands in the way, is ambition. I do not say that ambition is a bad thing in the worldly life, so long as its objects are not unworthy. If a man be a doctor or a lawyer, it is well that he should have the ambition to be a clever doctor or lawyer, in order that he may be able to do as much good as possible for his fellow-creatures in the profession which he has chosen for himself. But if the man's mind is so filled with ambition that there is no room for any other thought, that would be a bar against his being used for the transmission of higher forces. One cannot think of it as a sin; but the fact remains that it implies the continued presence in the various vehicles of a certain vibration, which will be out of harmony with any that the Master is likely to wish to send through.

Sensuality also is an absolute bar. It may be associated with actual wicked thought, or it may simply be a survival from the animal kingdom through which we have passed; in either case it creates a chronic disturbance and sets up a type of undulations which would be entirely inharmonious with any higher forces.

Those who desire to be ready for the Master's call must cast off these fetters; they must clear these difficulties out of the way. Though it is simple enough to understand what is required, it is not easy to do it. The mere study of Theosophy presents no serious difficulties; with a little assiduity one may obtain a mass of information about planes and sub-planes, about rings and rounds and planetary chains; but that is not enough. What is required is an attitude towards life — an attitude of benevolent philosophic calm. I had an old nurse who, when anything went wrong, used to say:

"Don't mind; it will be all the same a hundred years hence."

And really, you know, if one thinks of it, that is true. If some sorrow or sickness comes, it is very hard for the moment, but think how you will look back upon it from the heaven-life. Someone says something nasty about you; a hundred years hence it will not matter what he said. Except to himself it does not matter even now; why should you worry yourself about it? It is the custom to grow angry if someone speaks ill of one; but it is a bad custom. It is the fashion to let the astral body be disturbed under such circumstances, but it is a silly fashion; why should we follow it? If a man has been so wicked as to speak unkindly and untruly, it is he who will suffer for the wrong he has done; why should we unnecessarily allow our astral bodies to cause us suffering also?

What we do to others — that matters much to us, because it involves our responsibility; but as to what others do to us, what happens to us in the way of fortune or misfortune from without, we may say quite coolly in the words of the Californian philosopher:

"Nothing matters much; most things don't matter at all."

We must become indifferent to praise and blame, yet keenly alert for any opportunity of being useful. We must regard everything from the platform of universal brotherhood, trying always to see the good in everybody and everything, because to look for and to emphasize the good is a sure way of intensifying its action and evoking more good.

The man who adopts that attitude will make progress, for he will have plenty of force to spare for good work. The ordinary man of the world wastes nearly all his force in personal feelings — in taking offence, in annoyance, in envy, in jealousy; and so he has little left for unselfish purposes. It is the man who forgets himself who will be remembered by the Master. When the Master sees that he has worked steadily and selflessly for some years, and seems likely to be steadfast, He may examine him with regard to his fitness for apprenticeship. A Master takes a fully-accepted pupil into such close relationship with Himself that the standard of fitness must necessarily be high; and that is why the probationary stage is often a long one. Before the Master can take a man as part of Himself, there must be in that man no thoughts and no feelings which the Master could not tolerate within Himself — not because of His disgust for them, but because they would interfere with the work. Sometimes a member says: "I am deeply in earnest, and anxious to serve; I have worked and studied for years; why does not the Master accept me?"

The only reply we can give is:

"My dear sir, you are the man who ought to know that. What quality have you within you which would hinder a Master in His work? Besides, the question is never why should not a Master accept a man, but why should He? What is there in the man which makes him worthy of so high an honor?"

But when, as I have said, a man has worked well for some years, when it seems reasonably certain that he will remain steadfast and loyal, it may be that one day a Master will say to one of His pupils:

"So-and-so is a good man; bring him to me to-night."

That means that the Master will accept him on probation, and will keep him closely under His eye. The average length of that probation is seven years, but it may be shortened or lengthened according to circumstances. It is well that on the physical plane the candidate should be near someone who is either an Initiate or an accepted pupil, for in that way he may learn much. Through such an one he may receive occasionally a rare encouraging word from the Master; the attitude and daily life of the older pupil may give him many a hint as to what his own should be. It is not often the doing of any one brilliant action that brings a man to the feet of the Master; the message comes usually to one who is working away and not thinking of it.

There are many different Masters, and some candidates find themselves drawn to one of these Great Ones, and some to another. It does not matter; all are members of the same Great Brotherhood and all are engaged in the same glorious work. Sometimes the strongest attraction of the candidate is to one of the more advanced pupils instead of to a Master — because the pupil, whom he has seen and knows, is more real to him than a Master whom he has not consciously met. That usually means that when that more advanced pupil becomes an Adept in some future life, the candidate will wish to be his pupil. But if such a candidate is fit for acceptance before his chosen teacher has taken the Initiation which enables him to accept him, that teacher's Master will accept the candidate provisionally, and look after him until such time as the pupil is able to take him in hand. Meantime the Master will work upon him principally through the pupil whom he loves; and thus his teaching will come along the line of his strongest affection.

The Theosophical Society is drawing towards the end of its thirty-eighth year; and much fruit of its long labor is even already showing. The results of its work in the outer world are patent to all, but it has not been without certain inner results, which are not so generally known. Through it a number of students have drawn near to the Great Brotherhood to which it owes its inception, and have proved for themselves the truth of the teaching which it has given to them. Of our great Founder, Madame Blavatsky, who endured so much of toil and suffering that she might bring the Light to us, it may be said that she has seen of the travail of her soul, and has been satisfied. Yet it seems to us that her crown should shine yet more gloriously — that even more of those who owe their progress to her should be treading the Path, which she trod. The Gate stands open as of old; who will they be who shall qualify themselves to enter?

BUDDHIC CONSCIOUSNESS

All students are theoretically acquainted with the idea of the buddhic plane and its wonderful characteristic of unity of consciousness; but most of them probably regard the possibility of obtaining any personal experience of that consciousness as belonging to the far-distant future. The full development of the buddhic vehicle is for most of us still remote, for it belongs to the stage of the Fourth, or Arhat, Initiation; but it is perhaps not entirely impossible for those who are as yet far from that level to gain some touch of that higher type of consciousness in quite another way.

I was myself brought along what I should describe as the ordinary and commonplace line of occult development, and I had to fight my way laboriously upward, conquering one subplane after another, first in the astral world, then in the mental, and then in the buddhic; which means that I had a full use of my astral, mental and causal vehicles before anything came to me that I could define certainly as a real buddhic experience. This method is slow and toilsome, though I think it has its advantages in developing accuracy in observation, in making sure of each step before the next is taken. I have no doubt whatever that it was the best for a person of my temperament; indeed, it was probably the only way possible for me; but it does not follow that other people may not have quite other opportunities.

It has happened to me in the course of my work to come into contact with a number of those who are undergoing occult training; and perhaps the fact which emerges most prominently from my experience in that direction in the marvelous variety of method employed by our Masters. So closely adapted is the training to the individual that in no two cases is it the same; not only has every Master His own plan, but the same Master adopts a different scheme for each pupil, and so each person is brought along exactly that line which is most suitable for him.

A remarkable instance of this variability of method came under my notice not long ago, and I think that an explanation of it may perhaps be useful to some of our students. Let me first remind them of the curious inverted way in which the ego is reflected in the personality; the higher manas, or intellect, images itself in the mental body, the intuition, or buddhi, reflects itself in the astral body, and the spirit, or atma, itself somehow corresponds to the physical. These correspondences show themselves in the three methods of individualization, and they play their part in certain inner developments; but until lately it had not occurred to me that they could be turned to practical account at a much earlier stage by the aspirant for the occult progress.

A certain student of deeply affectionate nature developed (*as it was quite right and proper that he should*) an intense love for the teacher who had been appointed by his Master to assist him in the preliminary training. He made it a daily practice to form a strong mental image of that teacher, and then pour out his love upon him with all his force, thereby flooding his own astral body with crimson, and temporarily increasing its size enormously. He used to call the process "enlarging his aura". He showed such remarkable aptitude in this exercise, and it was so obviously beneficial to him, that an additional effort along the same line was suggested to him. He was recommended, while holding the image clearly before him, and sending out the love-force as strongly as ever, to try to raise his consciousness to a higher level and unify it with that of his teacher.

His first attempt to do this was amazingly successful. He described a sensation as of actually rising through space; he found what he supposed to be the sky like a roof barring his way, but the force of his will seemed to form a sort of cone in it, which presently became a tube through which he found himself rushing. He emerged into a region of blinding light, which was at the same time a sea of bliss so overwhelming that he could find no words to describe it. It was not in the least like anything that he had ever felt before; it grasped him as definitely and instantaneously as a giant hand might have done, and permeated his whole nature in a moment like a flood of electricity. It was more real than any physical object that he had ever seen, and yet at the same time so utterly spiritual. "It was as though God had taken me into Himself, and I felt His Life running through me", he said.

He gradually recovered himself and was able to examine his condition; and as he did so he began to realize that his consciousness was no longer limited as it had hitherto been — that he was somehow simultaneously present at every point of that marvelous sea of light; indeed, that in some inexplicable way he was himself that sea, even though apparently at the same time he was a point floating in it. It seemed to us who heard that he was groping after words to express the consciousness, which, as Madame Blavatsky so well puts it, has "its center everywhere and its circumference nowhere".

Further realization revealed to him that he had succeeded in his effort to become one with the consciousness of his teacher. He found himself thoroughly comprehending and sharing that teacher's feelings, and possessing a far wider and higher outlook on life than he had ever had before. One thing that impressed him immensely was the image of himself as seen through the teacher's eyes; it filled him with a sense of unworthiness, and yet of high resolve; as he whimsically put it.

"I found myself loving myself through my teacher's intense love for me, and I knew that I could and would make myself worthy of it".

He sensed also a depth of devotion and reverence which he had never before reached; he knew that in becoming one with his earthly teacher he had also entered the shrine of his true Master, with whom that teacher in turn was one, and he dimly felt himself in touch with a Consciousness of unrealizable splendor. But here his strength failed him; he seemed to slide down to his tube again, and opened his eyes upon the physical plane.

Consulted as to this transcendent experience, I enquired minutely into it, and easily satisfied myself that it was unquestionably an entry into the buddhic world, not by toilsome progress through the various stages of mental, but by a direct course along the ray of reflection from the highest astral subplane to the lowest of that intuitional world. I asked as to physical effects, and found that there were absolutely none; the student was in radiant health. So I recommended that he should repeat the effort, and that he should with utmost reverence try to press higher still, and to raise himself, if it might be, into that other August Consciousness. For I saw that here was a case of that combination of golden love and iron will that is so rare on this our Sorrowful Star; and I knew that a love which is utterly unselfish and a will which recognizes no obstacles may carry their possessor to the very Feet of God Himself.

The student repeated his experiment, and again he succeeded beyond all hope or expectation. He was able to enter that wider Consciousness, and he pressed onward and upward into it as though he were swimming out into some vast lake. Much of what he brought back with him he could not comprehend; shreds of ineffable glories, fragments of conceptions so vast and so gorgeous that no merely human mind can grasp them in their totality. But he gained a new idea of what love and devotion could be — an ideal after which to strive for the rest of his life.

Day after day he continued his efforts (*we found that once a day was as often as he could be wisely attempted*); further and further he penetrated into that great lake of love, and yet found no end to it. But gradually he became aware of something far greater still; he somehow knew that this indescribable splendor was permeated by a subtler glory yet more inconceivably splendid, and he tried to raise himself into that. And when he succeeded, he knew by its characteristics that it was the Consciousness of the great World-Teacher Himself. In becoming one with his own earthly teacher he had inevitably joined himself to the consciousness of his Master, with whom that teacher was already united; and in this further marvelous experience he was but proving the close union which exists between that Master and the Bodhisattva, who in turn had taught Him.

Into that shoreless sea of Love and Compassion he plunges daily in his meditation, with such upliftment and strengthening for himself as may readily be imagined; but he can never reach its limits, for no mortal man can fathom such an ocean as that.

Striving ever to penetrate more deeply into this wondrous new realm which had so suddenly opened before him, he succeeded one day in reaching a yet further development — a bliss so much more intense, a feeling so much more profound, that it seemed to him at first as much higher than his first buddhic touch as that had been above his earlier astral experiences. He remarked: "If I did not know that it is impossible for me to attain it yet, I should say that this must be Nirvana."

In reality it was only the next subplane of the buddhic — the second from the bottom, and the sixth from the top; but his impression is significant as showing that not only does consciousness widen as we rise, but the rate at which it widens increases rapidly. Not only is progress accelerated, but the rate of such acceleration grows by geometrical progression. Now this student reaches that higher subplane daily and as a matter of course, and is working vigorously and perseveringly in the hopes of advancing still farther. And the power, the balance and the certainty, which this introduces into his daily physical life is amazing and beautiful to see.

Another phenomenon, which he observes, as accompanying this, is that the intense bliss of that higher plane now persists beyond the time of meditation and is becoming more and more a part of his whole life. At first this persistence was for some twenty minutes after each meditation; then it reached an hour; then two hours; and he is confidently looking forward to a time when it will be his as a permanent possession — a part of himself. A remarkable feature of the case is that this prodigious daily exaltation is not followed by any sign of the slightest reaction or depression, but instead produces an ever-augmenting radiance and sunniness.

Becoming gradually more accustomed to functioning in this higher and more glorious world, he began to look about him to some extent, and was presently able to identify himself with many other less exalted consciousnesses. He found these existing as points within his extended self, and he discovered that by focusing himself at any of these points he could at once realize the highest qualities and spiritual aspirations of the person whom is represented. Seeking for a more detailed sympathy with some whom he knew and loved, he discerned that these points of consciousness were also, as he put it, holes through which he could pour himself down into their lower vehicles; and thus he came into touch with those parts of their lives and dispositions which could find no expression on the buddhic plane. This gave him a sympathy with their characters, a comprehension of their weaknesses, which was truly remarkable, and could probably have been attained in no other way — a most valuable quality for the work of a disciple in the future.

The wondrous unity of that intuitional world manifested itself to him in unsuspected examples. Holding in his hand one day what he regarded as specially beautiful little object, part of which was white, he fell into a sort of ecstasy of admiration of its graceful form and harmonious coloring. Suddenly, through the object, as he gazed at it, he saw unfolded before him a landscape, just as though the object had become a tiny window, or perhaps a crystal. The landscape is one that he knows and loves well, but there was no obvious reason why the little object should bring thus before him. A curious feature was that the white part of that object was represented in the sky of his picture. Impressed by this wholly unexpected phenomenon, he tried the experiment of raising his consciousness while he reveled in the beauty of the prospect. He had the sensation of passing through some resisting medium into a higher plane, and found that the view before him had changed to one, which was strange to him, but even more beautiful than that which he knew so well. The piles of white cloud had become towering snow-covered mountain, with its long line sweeping down to a sea of color richer than any that in this incarnation he has seen. The rocky bays, the buildings, the vegetation, were all foreign to him, though well-known to me; and by a little careful questioning I soon ascertained without room for doubt that the scene upon which he was looking was that which I suspected — a real physical view, but one many thousands of miles from the spot where he sat gazing at it. Since that hallowed spot is often in my mind, though I assuredly was not thinking of it at that moment, what the student saw may have been a thought-form of mine. I imagine that up to this point what had happened may be quite simply described. I presume that the student's emotion was excited by his admiration, and that the heightened vibrations which were caused in this way brought into operation his astral senses, and this enabled him to see a view which was not physically visible, but well within astral reach. The endeavor to press on further temporarily opened the mental sense, and by it he was able to see my thought-form — if that second view was a thought-form of mine.

But the student did not rest satisfied with that: he repeated his attempt to push on still higher, or (*as he put it*) still deeper into the real meaning of it all. Once more he had the experience of breaking through into some exalted and more refined state of matter; and this time it was no earthly scene that rewarded his effort, for the foreground burgeoned forth into an illimitable universe filled with masses of splendid color, pulsating with glorious life, and the snow-cowered mountain became a great White Throne vaster than any mountain, veiled in dazzling golden light. A strange fact connected with this vision is that the student to whom the experience came is entirely unacquainted with the Christian Scripture, and was unaware that any text existing therein had any bearing upon what he saw. I asked him whether he could repeat this experience at will; he did not know, but later on he tried the experiment, and succeeded in again passing through those stages in the same order, giving some additional details of the foreign landscape which proved to me that this was not merely a feat of memory; and this time the awe-stricken seer whispered that amidst the coruscations of that light he once had a passing glimpse of the outline of a Mighty Figure Who sat upon the Throne. This also, you may say, might be a thought-form, built by some Christian of vivid imagination. Perhaps; but when a few days later an opportunity occurred, and I asked a Wise One what signification we might attach to such a vision, He replied:

"Do you not see that, as there is but One Love, so there is but One Beauty? Whatever is beautiful, on any plane, is so because it is pushed back far enough, its connection will become manifest. All Beauty is of God, as all Love is of God; and through these, His Qualities, the pure in heart may always reach him".

Our students would do well to weigh these words, and follow out the idea contained in them. All beauty, whether it be of form or of color, whether it be in nature or in the human frame, in high achievements of art or in the humblest household utensil, is but an expression of the One Beauty and therefore in even the lowliest thing that is beautiful all beauty is implicitly contained, and so through it all beauty may be realized, and He Who Himself is Beauty may be reached. To understand this fully needs the buddhic consciousness by which our student arrived at its realization; but even at much lower levels the idea may be useful and fruitful.

I fully admit that the student whose experiences I have been relating is exceptional — that he possesses a strength of will, a power of love, a purity of heart and an utter unselfishness which are, unfortunately, far from common. Nevertheless, what he has done with such marked success may surely be copied to some extent by others less gifted. He has unfolded his consciousness upon a plane which is not normally reached by aspirants; he is rapidly building for himself a capable and most valuable vehicle there — for that is the meaning of the ever increasing persistence of sense of bliss and power. That this is a definite line of progress, and not a mere isolated example, is shown by the fact that even already the abnormal buddhic development is producing its effect upon the apparently neglected causal and mental bodies, stimulating them into action from above instead of leaving them to be laboriously influenced from below as usual. All this success is the result of steady effort along the line, which I have described.

"Go thou and do likewise". No harm can come to any man from an earnest endeavor to increase his power of love, his power of devotion, and his power to appreciate beauty; and by such endeavor it is at least possible that he may attain a progress of which he had not dreamed. Only be it remembered that, in this path as in every other, growth is achieved only by him who desires it not for his own sake but for sake of service. Forgetfulness of self and an eager desire to help others are the most prominent characteristics of the student whose inner story I have here told; these characteristics must be equally prominent in any who aspire to follow his example; without them no such consummation is possible.

TO THOSE WHO MOURN

Never the spirit was born; the spirit shall cease to be never;
Never was time it was not; End and Beginning are dreams!
Birthless and deathless and changeless remaineth the spirit forever;
Death hath not touched it at all, dead though the house of it seems!
-Sir Edwin Arnold

'Tis but as when one layeth
His worn-out robes away
And taking new ones, sayeth
"These will I wear today!"
So putteth by the Spirit
Lightly its garb of flesh,
And passeth to inherit
A residence afresh
-Sir Edwin Arnold

Friend: You have lost by death one whom you loved dearly, one who perhaps was all the world to you; and so to you that world seems empty, and life no longer worth the living. You feel that joy has left you forever, that existence can be for you henceforth nothing but hopeless sadness, naught but one aching longing for "the touch of a vanished hand and the sound of a voice that is still." You are thinking chiefly of yourself and your intolerable loss; but there is also another sorrow. Your grief is aggravated by your uncertainty as to the present condition of your beloved; you feel that he has gone, you know not where. You hope earnestly that all is well with him, but when you look upward all is void; when you cry there is no answer. And so despair and doubt overwhelm you, and make a cloud that hides from you the sun that never sets.

Your feeling is most natural; I, who write, understand it perfectly, and my heart is full of sympathy for all those who are afflicted as you are. But I hope that I can do more than sympathize: I hope that I can bring you help and relief. Such help and relief have come to thousands who were in your sad case. Why should they not come to you also?

You say: "How can there be relief or hope for me?"

There is the hope of relief for you because your sorrow is founded in misapprehension; you are grieving for something, *which has not really happened*. When you understand the *facts* you will cease to grieve.

You answer: "My loss is a fact. How can you help me, unless indeed you give me back my dead?"

I understand your feeling perfectly; yet bear with me for a while, and try to grasp three main propositions, which I am about to put before you, at first merely as broad statement, and then in convincing detail:

1. Your loss is only an *apparent fact*, apparent from your point of view. I want to bring you to another viewpoint. Your suffering is the result of a great delusion, of ignorance of Nature's law; let me help you on the road towards knowledge by explaining a few simple truths, which you can study further at your leisure.

2. You need be under no uneasiness or uncertainty with regard to the condition of your loved one, for the life after death is no longer a mystery. The world beyond the grave exists under the same natural laws as this, which we know, and has been explored and examined with scientific accuracy.

3. You must not mourn, for your mourning does harm to your loved one. If you can once open your mind to the truth, you will mourn no more.

You may perhaps feel that these are only assertions; but let me ask you on what grounds you hold your present belief, whatever it may be. You think you hold it because some Church teaches it, or because it is supposed to be founded upon what is written in some holy book; or because it is the general belief of those around you, the accepted opinion of your time. But if you will try to clear your mind from preconceptions, you will see that this opinion also rests merely upon assertion for the Churches teach different views, and the words of the holy book may be and have been variously interpreted. The accepted view of your time is *not* based upon any definite knowledge; it is mere hearsay. These matters, which affect us so nearly and so deeply are too important to be left to mere supposition or vague belief; they demand the certainty of scientific investigation and tabulation. Such investigation has been undertaken, such tabulation has been accomplished; and it is the result of these, which I wish to put before you. I ask no blind credence; I state what I myself know to be facts, and I invite you to examine them.

Let us consider these propositions one by one. To make the subject clear to you I must tell you a little more about the constitution of man than is generally known to those who have made no special study of the matter. You have heard it said vaguely that man possesses an immortal something called a soul, which is supposed to survive the death of the body. I want you to cast aside that vagueness and to understand that, even if it were true, it is an understatement of the facts. Do not say: "I hope that I have a soul," but "I *know* that I *am* a soul." For that is the real truth; man *is* a soul, and *has* a body. The body is not the man; it is only the clothing of the man. What you call death is the laying aside of a worn-out garment, and it is no more the end of the man than it is the end of *you* when you remove your overcoat. Therefore you have *not* lost your friend; you have only lost sight of the cloak in which you were accustomed to see him. The cloak is gone, but the man who wore it is not; surely it is the *man* that you love and not the garment.

Before you can understand your friend's condition you must understand your own. Try to grasp the fact that you are an immortal being, immortal because you are divine in essence, because you are a spark from God's own Fire; that you lived for ages before you put on this vesture that you call a body, and that you will live for ages after it has crumbled into dust. "God made man to be an image of His own eternity." This is not a guess or a pious belief; it is a definite scientific fact, capable of proof, as you may see from the literature on the subject if you will take the trouble to read.

What you have been thinking of as your life is in truth only one day of your life as a soul, and the same is true of your beloved; therefore *he is not dead*. It is only his body that is cast aside.

Yet you must not therefore think of him as a mere bodiless breath, as in any way less himself than he was before. As St Paul said long ago: "There is a natural body, and there is a spiritual body." People misunderstand that remark, because they think of these bodies as successive, and do not realize that we, all of us, possess both of them even now. You, as you read this, have both a "natural" or physical body, and one which you cannot see, that which St. Paul called the "spiritual." And when you lay aside the physical you still retain that other finer vehicle; you are clothed in your "spiritual body." If we symbolize the physical body as an overcoat or cloak, we may think of this spiritual body as the ordinary house-coat which the man wears underneath that outer garment.

If that idea is by this time clear to you, let us advance another step. It is not only at what you call death that you doff that overcoat of dense matter; every night when you go to sleep you slip it off for awhile, and roam about the world in your spiritual body, invisible as far as this dense world is concerned, but clearly visible to those friends who happen to be using their spiritual bodies at the same time. For each body sees only that which is on its own level; your physical body sees only other physical bodies. When you resume your overcoat that is to say, when you come back to your denser body, it occasionally happens that you have some recollection, although usually a considerably distorted one of what you have seen when you were away elsewhere; and then you call it a vivid dream. Sleep, then, may be described as a kind of temporary death, the difference being that you do not withdraw yourself so entirely from your overcoat as to be unable to resume it. It follows that when you sleep, you enter the same condition as that into which your beloved has passed. What that condition is I will now proceed to explain.

Many theories have been current as to the life after death, most of them based upon misunderstandings of ancient scriptures. At one time the horrible dogma of what was called everlasting punishment was almost universally accepted in Europe, though none but the hopelessly ignorant believe it now. It was based upon a mistranslation of certain words attributed to Christ, and it was maintained by the mediaeval monks as a convenient bogey with which to frighten the ignorant masses into well-doing. As the world advanced in civilization, men began to see that such a tenet was not only blasphemous but ridiculous. Modern religionists have therefore replaced it by somewhat saner suggestions; but they are usually quite vague and far from the simplicity of the truth. All the Churches have complicated their doctrines because they insisted upon starting with an absurd and unfounded dogma of a cruel and angry Deity who wished to injure His people. They import this dreadful doctrine from primitive Judaism, instead of accepting the teaching of the Christ that God is a loving Father. People who have grasped the fundamental fact that God is Love, and that His universe is governed by wise eternal laws have begun to realize that those laws must be obeyed in the world beyond the grave just as much as in this. But even yet beliefs are vague. We are told of a faraway heaven, of a day of judgment in the remote future, but little information is given us as to what happens here and now. Those who teach do not even pretend to have any personal experience of after-death conditions. They tell us not what they themselves know, but only what they have heard from others. How can that satisfy us?

The truth is that the day of blind belief is past; the era of scientific knowledge is with us, and we can no longer accept ideas unsustained by reason and common sense. There is no reason why scientific methods should not be applied to the elucidation of problems which in earlier days were left entirely to religion; indeed, *such methods have been applied* by The Theosophical Society and the Society of Psychical Research; and it is the result of these investigations, made in a scientific spirit, that I wish to place before you now.

We are spirits, but we live in a material world, a world, however, which is only partially known to us. All the information that we have about it comes to us through our senses; but these senses are seriously imperfect. Solid objects we can see; we can usually see liquids, unless they are perfectly clear; but gases are in most cases invisible to us. Research shows that there are other kinds of matter far finer than the rarest of gases; but to these our physical senses do not respond, and so we can gain no information with regard to them by physical means.

Nevertheless, we can come into touch with them; we can investigate them, but we can do it only by means of that "Spiritual body" to which reference has been made, for that has its senses just as this one has. Most men have not yet learned how to use them, but this is a power, which can be acquired by man. We know that it can be, because it has been so acquired; and those who have gained it find themselves able to see much, which is hidden from the view of the ordinary man. They learn that this world of ours is far more wonderful than we have ever supposed; that though men have been living in it for thousands of years, most of them have remained blankly ignorant of all the higher and more beautiful parts of its life. The line of research to which I am referring has already yielded many marvelous results, and is opening before us new vistas every day. This information may be gleaned from Theosophical literature, but we are here concerned with only one part of it, with the new knowledge that it puts before us as to the life beyond what we call death, and the condition of those who are enjoying it.

The first thing that we learn is that death is not the end of life, as we have ignorantly assumed, but is only a step from one stage of life to another. I have already said that it is the laying aside of an overcoat, but that after it the man still finds himself clad in his ordinary housecoat, the spiritual body. But though, because it is so much finer, St Paul gave it the name of "spiritual," it is still a body, and therefore, material, even though the matter of which it is composed be very much finer than ordinarily known to us. The physical body serves the spirit as a means of communication with the physical world. Without that body as an instrument, he would be unable to communicate with that world, to impress himself upon it or to receive impressions from it. We find that the spiritual body serves exactly the same purpose; it acts as an intermediary for the spirit with the higher and "spiritual" world. But this spiritual world is not something vague, faraway and unattainable; it is simply a higher part of the world, which we now inhabit. I am not for a moment denying that there are other worlds, far higher and more remote; I am saying only that what is commonly called death has nothing to do with those, and that it is merely a transference from one stage or condition to another in this world with which we are all familiar. It may be said that the man who makes this change becomes invisible to you; but if you think of it, you will see that the man has always been invisible to you, that what you have been in the habit of seeing is only the body which he inhabited. Now he inhabits another and a finer body, which is beyond your ordinary sight, but not necessarily by any means beyond your reach.

The first point to realize is that those whom we call the dead have not left us. We have been brought up in a complex belief which implies that every death is a separate and marvelous miracle, that when the soul leaves the body it somehow vanishes into a heaven beyond the stars, no suggestion being made as to the mechanical means of transit over the appalling spaces involved. Nature's processes are assuredly wonderful, and often to us incomprehensible, but they never fly in the face of reason and common sense. When you take off your overcoat in the hall, you do not suddenly vanish to some distant mountain-top; you are standing just where you were before, though you may present a different outward appearance. Precisely in the same way, when a man puts off his physical body he remains exactly where he was before. It is true that you no longer see him, but the reason for this is not that he has gone away, but that the body, which he is now wearing is not visible to your physical eyes.

You may be aware that our eyes respond only to a very small proportion of the vibrations, which exist in nature, and consequently the only substances which we can see are those which happen to reflect these particular undulations. The sight of your "spiritual body" is equally a matter of response to undulations, but they are of quite a different order, coming from a much finer type of matter. All this, if it interests you, you may find worked out in detail in Theosophical literature.

For the moment all which concerns us is that by means of your physical body you can see and touch the physical world only, while by means of the "spiritual body" you can see and touch the things of the spiritual world. And remember that this is in no sense *another* world, but simply a more refined part of this world. Once more I say, there are other worlds, but we are not concerned with them now. The man of whom you think as departed is in reality with you still. When you stand side by side, you in the physical body and he in the "spiritual" vehicle, you are unconscious of his presence because you cannot see him; but when you leave your physical body in sleep you stand side by side with him in full and perfect consciousness, and your union with him is in every way as full as it used to be. So during sleep you are happy with him whom you love; it is only during waking hours that you feel the separation.

Unfortunately for most of us, there is a break between the physical consciousness and the consciousness of the spiritual body, so that although in the latter we can perfectly remember the former, many of us find it impossible to bring through into waking life the memory of what the soul does when it is away from the body in sleep. If this memory were perfect, for us there would indeed be no death. Some men have already attained this continued consciousness, and all may attain it by degrees, for it is part of the natural unfolding of the powers of the soul. In many, such unfolding had already begun, and so fragments of memory come through, but there is a tendency to stamp them as only dreams and therefore valueless, a tendency specially prevalent among those who have made no study of dreams and do not understand what they really are. But while as yet only a few possess full sight and full memory, there are many who have been able to feel the presence of their loved ones, even though they cannot see; and there are others who though they have no definite memory, wake from slumber with a sense of peace and blessedness which is the result of what has happened in that higher world.

Remember always that this is the lower world and that is the higher, and that the greater in this case includes the less. In that consciousness you remember perfectly what has happened in this, because as you pass from this to that in falling asleep, you are casting off a hindrance, the encumbrance of the lower body; but when you come back to this lower life, you again assume that burden, and in assuming it you cloud the higher faculties and so lapse into forgetfulness. So it follows that if you have some piece of news that you wish to give to a departed friend, you have only to formulate it clearly in your mind before falling asleep, with the resolution that you will tell him of it, and you are quite certain to do so as soon as you meet him. Sometimes you may wish to consult him on some point, and here the break between the two forms of consciousness usually prevents you from bringing back a clear answer. Yet even if you cannot bring back a definite recollection, you will often wake with a strong impression as to his wish or his decision; and you may usually take it that such an impression is correct. At the same time, you should consult him as little as possible, for, as we shall see later, it is distinctly undesirable that the dead should be troubled in their higher world with affairs that belong to the department of life from which they have been freed.

This brings us to the consideration of the life, which the dead are leading. In it there are many and great variations, but at least it is almost always happier than the earth life. As an old scripture puts it: "The souls of the righteous are in the hand of God, and there shall no torment touch them. In the sight of the universe they seem to die, and their departure is taken for misery, and their going from us to be utter destruction; but they are in peace." We must disabuse ourselves of antiquated theories; the dead man does not leap suddenly into an impossible heaven, nor does he fall into a still more impossible hell. There is indeed no hell in the old wicked sense of the word; and there is no hell anywhere in any sense except such as a man makes for himself. Try to understand clearly that death makes no change in the man; he does not suddenly become a great saint or angel, nor is he suddenly endowed with all the wisdom of the ages. He is just the same man after his death as he was the day before it, with the same emotions, the same dispositions, the same intellectual development. The only difference is that he has lost the physical body.

Try to think exactly what that means. It means absolute freedom from the possibility of pain or fatigue; freedom also from all irksome duties; entire liberty (*probably for the first time in his life*) to do exactly what he likes. In the physical life man is constantly under constraint; unless he is one of a small minority who have independent means he is ever under the necessity of working in order to obtain money, money which he must have in order to buy food and clothing and shelter for himself and for those who are dependent upon him. In a few rare instances, such as those of the artist and the musician, the man's work is a joy to him, but in most cases it is a form of labor to which he would certainly not devote himself unless he were compelled.

In this spiritual world no money is necessary, food and shelter are no longer needed, for its glory and its beauty are free to all its inhabitants without money and without price. In its rarefied matter, in the spiritual body, he can move hither and thither as he will. If he loves art he may spend the whole of his time in the contemplation of the masterpieces of all the greatest of men; if he be a musician, he may pass from one to the other of the world's chiefest orchestras, or may spend his time in listening to the most celebrated performers. Whatever has been his delight on earth, his hobby, as we should say, he has now the fullest liberty to devote himself to it entirely and to follow it out to the utmost, provided only that its enjoyment is that of the intellect or of the highest emotions, that its gratification does not necessitate the possession of a physical body. Thus it will be seen at once that all rational and decent men are infinitely happier after death than before it, for they have ample time not only for pleasure but for really satisfactory progress along the lines which interest them most.

Are there then none in that world who are unhappy? Yes, for that life is necessarily a sequel to this, and the man is in every respect the same man as he was before he left his body. If his enjoyments in this world were low and coarse, he will find himself unable to gratify his desires. A drunkard will suffer from unquenchable thirst, having no longer a body through which it can be assuaged; the glutton will miss the pleasures of the table; the miser will no longer find gold for his gathering. The man who has yielded himself during earth-life to unworthy passions will find them gnawing at his vitals. The sensualist still palpitates with cravings that can never now be satisfied; the jealous man is still torn by his jealousy, all the more than he can no longer interfere with the action of its object. Such people as these unquestionably do suffer, but only such as these, only those whose proclivities and passions have been coarse and physical in their nature. And even they have their fate absolutely in their own hands. They have but to conquer these inclinations, and they are at once free from the sufferings, which such longings entail. Remember always that there is no such thing as punishment; there is only the natural result of a definite cause; so that you have only to remove the cause and the effect ceases, not always immediately, but as soon as the energy of the cause is exhausted.

There are many people who have avoided these more glaring vices, yet have lived what may be called worldly lives, caring principally for society and its conventions, and thinking only of enjoying themselves. Such people as these have no active suffering in the spiritual world, but they often find it dull, they find time hanging heavy on their hands. They can foregather with others of their type, but they usually find them somewhat monotonous, now that there is no longer any competition in dress or in general ostentation, while the better and cleverer people whom they desire to reach are customarily otherwise engaged and therefore somewhat inaccessible to them. But any man who has rational intellectual or artistic interests will find himself quite infinitely happier outside his physical body than in it, and it must be remembered that it is always possible for a man to develop in that world a rational interest if he is wise enough to do so.

The artistic and intellectual are supremely happy in that new life; yet even happier still, I think, are those whose keenest interest has been in their fellow men, those whose greatest delight has been to help, to succor, to teach. For though in that world there is no longer any hunger or thirst or cold, there are still those who are in sorrow who can be comforted; those who are in ignorance who can be taught. Just because in western countries there is so little knowledge of the world beyond the grave, we find in that world many who need instruction as to the possibilities of this new life; and so one who knows may go about spreading hope and glad tidings there just as much as here. But remember always that "there" and "here" are only terms in deference to our blindness; for that world is here, close around us all the time, and not for a moment to be thought of as a distant or difficult of approach.

Do the dead then see us? may be asked; do they hear what we say? Undoubtedly they see us in the sense that they are always conscious of our presence, that they know whether we are happy or miserable; but they do not hear the words we say, nor are they conscious in detail of our physical actions. A moment's thought will show us what are the limits of their power to see. They are inhabiting, what we have called the "spiritual body," a body which exists in ourselves, and is, as far as appearance goes, an exact duplicate of the physical body; but while we are awake our consciousness is focused exclusively in the latter. We have already said that just as only physical matter appeals to the physical body, so only the matter of the spiritual world is discernible by that higher body. Therefore, what the dead man can see of us is only our spiritual body, which, however, he has no difficulty in recognizing. When we are what we call asleep, our consciousness is using that vehicle, and so to the dead man we are awake; but when we transfer our consciousness to the physical body, it seems to the dead man that we fall asleep, because though he still sees us, we are no longer paying any attention to him or able to communicate with him. When a living friend falls asleep we are quite aware of his presence, but for the moment we cannot communicate with him. Precisely similar is the condition of the living man (*while he is awake*) in the eyes of the dead. Because we cannot usually remember in our waking consciousness what we have seen during sleep, we are under the delusion that we have lost our dead; but they are never under the delusion that they have lost us, because they can see us all the time. To them the only difference is that we are with them during the night and away from them during the day; whereas when they were on earth with us, exactly the reverse was the case.

Now this which, following St. Paul, we have been calling the "spiritual body" (*it is more usually spoken of as the astral body*) is especially the vehicle of our feelings and emotions; it is therefore these feelings and emotions of ours which show themselves most clearly to the eyes of the dead. If we are joyous, they instantly observe it, but they do not necessarily know the reason of the joy; if sadness comes over us, they at once realize it and share it, even though they may not know why we are sad. All this, of course, is during our waking hours; when we are asleep, they converse with us as of yore on earth. Here in our physical life we can dissemble our feelings; in that higher world this is impossible, for they show themselves instantly in visible change. Since so many of our thoughts are connected with our feelings, most of these also are readily obvious in that world; but anything in the nature of abstract thought is still hidden.

You still say that all this has little in common with the heaven and hell of which we are taught in our infancy; yet it is the fact that this is the reality, which lay behind these myths. Truly there is no hell; yet it will be seen that the drunkard or the sensualist may have prepared for himself something, which is no bad imitation thereof. Only it is not everlasting; it endures only until his desires have worn themselves out. He can at any moment put a period to it, if he is strong enough and wise enough to dominate those earthly cravings and to raise himself entirely above them. This is the truth underlying the Catholic doctrine of purgatory, the idea that after death the evil qualities have to be burned out of a man by a certain amount of suffering before he is capable of enjoying the bliss of heaven.

There is a second and higher stage of the life after death, which does correspond very closely to a rational conception of heaven. That higher level is attained when all lower or selfish longings have absolutely disappeared; then the man passes into a condition of religious ecstasy or of higher intellectual activity, according to the line along which his energy has flowed out during his earth-life. That is for him a period of the most supreme bliss, a period of far greater comprehension, or nearer approach to reality. But this joy comes to all, not only to the especially pious.

It must by no means be regarded as a reward, but once more only as the inevitable result of the character evolved in earth life. If a man is full of high and unselfish affection or devotion, if he is splendidly developed intellectually or artistically, the inevitable result of such development will be this enjoyment of which we are speaking. Be it remembered that all these are but stages of one life, and that just as a man's behavior during his youth makes for him to a large extent the conditions of his middle life and old age, so a man's behavior during his earth-life determines his condition during these after-states.

Is this state of bliss eternal? You ask. No, for, as I have said, it is the result of the earth life, and a finite cause can never produce an infinite result.

The life of man is far longer and far greater than you have supposed. The Spark, which has come forth from God must return to Him, and we are as yet far from that perfection of Divinity. All life is evolving, for evolution is God's law; and man grows slowly and steadily along with the rest. What is commonly called man's life is in reality only one day of his true and longer life. Just as in this ordinary life man rises each morning, puts on his clothes, and goes forth to do his daily work, and then when night descends he lays aside those clothes and takes his rest, and then again on the following morning rises afresh to take up his work at the point where he left it, just so when the man comes into physical life he puts upon him the vesture of the physical body, and when his work-time is over he lays aside that vesture again in what you call death, and passes into the more restful condition which I have described; and when that rest is over he puts upon himself once more the garment of the body and goes forth yet again to begin a new day of physical life, taking up his evolution at the point where he left it. And this long life of his lasts until he attains that goal of divinity, which God means him to attain.

All this may well be new to you, and because it is new it may seem strange and grotesque. Yet all that I have said is capable of proof, and has been tested many times over; but if you wish to read all this you must study the literature on the subject, for in a short pamphlet with a special purpose, such as this, I can merely state the facts, and not attempt to adduce the proofs.

You may perhaps ask whether the dead are not disturbed by anxiety for those whom they have left behind. Sometimes that does happen, and such anxiety delays their progress; so we should, as far as possible, avoid giving any occasion for it. The dead man should be utterly free from all thought of the life, which he has left, so that he may devote himself entirely to the new existence upon which he has entered. Those therefore who have in the past depended upon his advice should now endeavor to think for themselves, lest by still mentally depending upon him they should strengthen his ties with the world from which he has for the moment turned. So it is always an especially good deed to take care of children, whom a dead man leaves behind him, for in that way one not only benefits the children, but also relieves the departed parent from anxiety and helps him on his upward path.

If the dead man has during life been taught foolish and blasphemous religious doctrines, he sometimes suffers from anxiety with regard to his own future fate. Fortunately there are in the spiritual world many who make it their business to find men who are under such a delusion as this, and to set them free from it by a rational explanation of facts. Not only are there dead men who do this, but there are also many living men who devote their time during the sleep of the body each night to the service of the dead, endeavoring to relieve people from nervousness or suffering by explaining to them the truth in all its beauty. All suffering comes from ignorance; dispel the ignorance and the suffering is gone.

One of the saddest cases of apparent loss is when a child passes away from this physical world and its parents are left to watch its empty place, to miss its loving prattle. What then happens to children in this strange new spiritual world? Of all those who enter it, they are perhaps the happiest and the most entirely and immediately at home. Remember that they do not lose the parents, the brothers, the sisters, the playmates whom they love; it is simply that they have them to play with during what we call the night instead of the day; so that they have no feeling of loss or separation. During our day they are never left alone, for, as here children gather together and play together, play in Elysian fields full of rare delights. We know how a child here enjoys "making believe," pretending to be this character or that in history, playing the principal part in all sorts of wonderful fairy stories or tales of adventure. In the finer matter of that higher world, thoughts take to themselves visible form, and so the child who imagines himself a certain hero promptly takes on temporarily the actual appearance of that hero. If he wishes for an enchanted castle, his thought can build that enchanted castle. If he desires an army to command, all at once that army is there. And so among the dead the hosts of children are always full of joy, indeed, often even riotously happy.

And those other children of different disposition, those whose thoughts turn more naturally to religious matters, they also never fail to find that for which they long. For the angels and the saints of old exist, they are not mere pious fancies; and those who need them, those who believe in them are surely drawn to them, also find them kinder and more glorious than ever fancy dreamed. There are those who would find God Himself, God in material form; yet even they are not disappointed, for from the gentlest and the kindest teachers they learn that all forms are

God's forms, for He is everywhere, and those who would serve and help even the lowest of His creatures are truly serving and helping Him. Children love to be useful; they love to help and comfort; a wide field for such helping and comfort lies before them among the ignorant in the higher world, and as they move through its glorious fields on their errands of mercy and of love they learn the truth of the beautiful old teaching: "Inasmuch as ye have done it unto one of the least of these My brethren ye had done it unto Me."

And the tiny babies, those who are as yet too young to play? Have no fear for them, for many a dead mother waits eagerly to clasp them to her breast, to receive them and to love them as though they were her own. Usually such little ones rest in the spiritual world but a short time, and then return to earth once more, often to the very same father and mother. About these the mediaeval monk invented an especially cruel horror, in the suggestion that the un-baptized baby was lost to its friends forever. Baptism is a true sacrament, and not without its uses; but let no one be so unscientific as to imagine that the omission of an outward form like this can affect the working of God's eternal laws, or change Him from a God of love into a pitiless tyrant.

We have spoken so far only of the possibility of reaching the dead by rising to their level during sleep, which is the normal and natural way. There is also, of course, the abnormal and unnatural method of spiritualism, whereby for a moment the dead put on again the veil of flesh, and so become once more visible to our physical eyes. Students of occultism do not recommend this method, partly because it often holds back the dead in his evolution, and partly because there is so much uncertainty about it and so great a possibility of deception and personation. The subject is far too large to take up in a pamphlet such as this, but I have dealt with it in a book called *The Other Side of Death*. There also will be found some account of instances in which the dead spontaneously return to this lower world and manifest themselves in various ways, generally because they want us to do something for them. In all such cases it is best to try and find out, as speedily as may be, what they require, and fulfill their wishes, if possible, so that their minds may be at rest.

If you have been able to assimilate what I have already said, you will now understand that, however natural it may be for us to feel sorrow at the death of our relatives, that sorrow is an error and an evil, and we ought to overcome it. There is no need to sorrow for *them*, for they have passed into a far wider and happier life. If we sorrow for our own fancied separation from them, we are in the first place weeping over an illusion, for in truth they are not separated from us; and secondly, we are acting selfishly, because we are thinking more of our own apparent loss than of their great and real gain. We must strive to be utterly unselfish, as indeed all love should be. We must think of *them* and not of ourselves, not of what we wish or we feel, but solely of what is best for them and most helpful to their progress.

If we mourn, if we yield to gloom and depression, we throw out from ourselves a heavy cloud, which darkens the sky for *them*. Their very affection for us, their very sympathy for us, lay them open to this direful influence. We can use the power, which that affection gives us to help them instead of hindering them, if we only will, but to do that requires courage and sacrifice. We must forget ourselves utterly in our earnest and loving desire to be of the greatest possible assistance to our dead. Every thought, every feeling of ours influences them; let us then take care that there shall be no thought which is not broad and helpful, ennobling and purifying.

If it is probable that they may be feeling some anxiety about us, let us be persistently cheerful, that we may assure them that they have no need to feel troubled on our account. If, during physical life, they have been without detailed and accurate information as to the life after death, let us endeavor at once to assimilate such information ourselves, and to pass it on in our nightly conversations with them. Since our thoughts and feelings are so readily mirrored in theirs, let us see to it that those thoughts and feelings are always elevating and encouraging. "If ye know these things, blessed are ye if ye do them."

Try to comprehend the unity of all. There is one God, and all are one in Him. If we can bring home to ourselves the unity of that eternal Love, there will be no more sorrow for us; for we shall realize, not for ourselves alone but for those whom we love, that whether we live or die, we are the Lord's and that in Him we live and move and have our being, whether it be in this world or in the world to come. The attitude of mourning is a fruitless attitude, an ignorant attitude. The more we know, the more fully we shall trust, for we shall feel with utter certainty that we and our dead are alike in the hands of perfect Power and perfect Wisdom directed by perfect Love.

THE HIDDEN SIDE OF LODGE MEETINGS

Let us consider the hidden side of a meeting of a Theosophical Lodge; more specifically, the ordinary weekly meeting at which the Lodge is following a definite line of study. I am, of course, referring only to the meetings of members of the Lodge for the occult effect, which I wish to describe is entirely impossible in connection with any meetings to which non-members are admitted.

Naturally the work of every Lodge has its public side. There are lectures given to the public, and opportunities offered for them to ask questions; all this is good and necessary. But every Lodge which is worthy on the name is also doing something far higher than any work on the physical plane, and this higher work can only be done in its own primary meetings.

Furthermore it can be done only if these meetings are properly conducted and entirely harmonious. If the members are thinking of themselves in any way—if they have personal vanity such as might show itself in the desire to shine or to take a prominent part in the proceedings; if they have other personal feeling, so that they take offence or are affected by envy or jealousy, no useful occult effect can possibly be produced. But if they have forgotten themselves in the earnest endeavor to understand the subject appointed for study, a very considerable and beneficial result, of which they usually have no conception, may very readily be produced. Let me explain the reason of this.

We will assume a series of meetings at which a certain book is being used for study. Every member knows beforehand what paragraph or page will be taken at the meeting, and it is expected that he will not come to that meeting without previous preparation. He must not be in the attitude of a nestling waiting with open mouth and expecting that someone else will feed him; on the contrary, every member should have an intelligent grasp of the subject which is to be considered, and should be prepared to contribute his share of information. A good plan is for each member of the circle to make himself responsible for the examination of certain of our theosophical books.

The subject to be considered at the meeting should have been announced at the previous one, and each member should make himself responsible for looking carefully through the book or books committed to his charge for any reference to it, so that when he comes to the meeting he is already possessed of any information about it which is contained in that particular book, and is prepared to contribute this when called upon. In this way every member has his work to do, and each is greatly helped to a full and clear comprehension of the matter under consideration when all present are thus earnestly fixing their thought upon it. In order to grasp this fully let us think for a moment of the effect of a thought.

Every thought which is sufficiently definite to be worthy of the name produces two separate results. First, it is itself a vibration of the mental body, and it may take place at different levels in that body. Like every other vibration it tends to reproduce itself in surrounding matter. Just as a harp string when set in vibration communicates that vibration to the air about it, thus making an audible sound, so the thought vibration established in matter of a certain density within a person's mental body communicates itself to matter of the same density in the mental plane, which surrounds him.

Secondly, each thought draws round itself the living matter of the mental plane and builds itself a vehicle which we call a thought-form. If the thought is simply an exercise of the intellect (*such as might be involved in the working out of a mathematical or geometrical problem*) the thought-form remains on mental levels; but if it is in the least tinged with desire or emotion, or if it is in any way connected with the personal self, it at once draws round itself a vesture of astral matter as well, and manifests itself upon the astral plane.

An intense effort at the realization of the abstract —an attempt to comprehend what is meant by the fourth dimension or by the 'tabularity' of the table, for example—means an activity upon the higher mental levels; while if the thought is mingled with unselfish affection, high aspiration or devotion, it is even possible that a vibration upon the buddhic plane may enter into it and multiply its power a hundredfold. We must consider these two results separately and see what follows from each of them.

The vibration may be thought of as spreading on the mental plane through matter capable of responding to it—'that is to say, through matter of the same degree of density as that in which it was originally generated. Radiating in this way it naturally comes into contact with the mental bodies of many other people, and its tendency is to reproduce itself in these bodies. The distance to which it can radiate effectively depends partly upon the nature of the vibration and partly upon the opposition which it meets. Vibrations entangled with the lower types of astral matter may be deflected or overwhelmed by a multitude of other vibrations at the same level, just as in the midst of the roar of a great city a soft sound will be entirely drowned.

The ordinary self-centered thought of the average man begins on the lowest of the mental levels and instantly plunges down to correspondingly low levels of the astral. Its power in both planes is therefore very limited because, however violent it may be, there is such an immense and turbulent sea of similar thought surging all around that the vibrations are very soon lost and overpowered in the confusion.

A vibration generated at a higher level, however, has a much clearer field for its action, because at present the number of thoughts producing such a vibration is very small—indeed theosophical thought is almost in a class by itself from this point of view. There are truly religious people whose thought is quite as elevated as ours, but it is never so precise and definite; there are large numbers of people whose thoughts on matters of business and money-making are as precise as could be desired, but they are not elevated or altruistic. Even scientific thought is scarcely ever in the same class as that of the true Theosophist, so that our students may be said to have a field to themselves the mental world.

The result of this is that when a man thinks on theosophical subjects he is sending out all around him a vibration which is very powerful because it is practically unopposed, like a sound in the midst of a vast silence, or a light shining forth on the darkest night. It sets in motion a level of mental matter which is as yet very rarely used, and the radiations which are caused by it impinge upon the mental body of the average man at a point where it is quite dormant.

This gives to the thought its peculiar value, not only to the thinker but to others around him; for its tendency is to awaken and to bring into use an entirely new part of the thinking apparatus. It must be understood that such a vibration does not necessarily convey theosophical thought to those who are ignorant of it; but in awakening this higher portion of the mental body, it undoubtedly tends to elevate and liberalize the person's thought as a whole, along whatever lines it may be in the habit of moving, and in this way produces an incalculable benefit.

If the thought of a single person produces these results, it will be readily understood that the thought of twenty or thirty directed to the same subject will achieve an effort enormously greater. The power of the united thought of a number of people is far more than the sum of their separate thoughts; it would be much more nearly represented by their product. So it will be seen that, even from this point of view alone, it is a very good thing for any city or community that a Theosophical Lodge should be regularly meeting in its midst, since its proceedings—if they are conducted in the proper spirit—cannot but have a distinctly elevating and ennobling effect upon the thought of the surrounding population. Naturally there will be many people whose minds cannot yet be awakened at all upon those higher levels: but even for them the constant beating of the waves of this more advanced thought will bring nearer the time of their awakening.

Nor must we forget the result produced by the formation of definite thought-forms. These also will be radiated from the center of activity, but they can affect only such minds as are already to some extent responsive to ideas of this nature. In these days there are many such minds, and there are members who can attest to the fact that after they have been discussing a question such as reincarnation it not infrequently happens that they are asked for information upon that very subject by persons whom they had not previously supposed to be interested in it. It should be observed that the thought-form is capable of conveying the exact nature of the thought to those who are somewhat prepared to receive it, whereas the thought vibration, though it reaches a far wider circle, is much less definite in its action.

It can be seen, then, that a momentous effect upon the mental plane is produced quite unintentionally by our members in the ordinary course of their study—something far greater, in reality, than their intentional efforts in the way of propaganda are ever likely to produce. But this is not all, for by far the most important part is yet to come. Every Lodge of the Society is a center of interest to the Great Masters of Wisdom, and when it works loyally their thoughts and those of their pupils are frequently turned towards it. In this way a force much greater than our own often shines out from our gatherings, and an influence of inestimable value may be focused where, so far as we know, it would not otherwise rest.

This may, indeed, seem the limit, which our work can attain, yet there is something even greater. All students of the occult are aware that the light and life of the Logos flood the whole of his system — that on every plane is outpoured that special manifestation of his strength that is appropriate to it. Naturally the higher the plane the less veiled is his glory, because as we ascend we are drawing nearer to its source. Normally the force outpoured in each plane is strictly limited to it; but it can descend into and illuminate a lower plane if a special channel is prepared for it.

Such a channel is always provided whenever any thought or feeling has an entirely unselfish aspect. A selfish emotion moves in a closed curve and so brings its own response on its own plane; an utterly unselfish motion is an outrush of energy which does not return, but in its own upward movement provides a channel for a down pouring of divine power from the plane next above. This is the reality lying behind the old idea of an answer to prayer.

The man who is occupied in the earnest study of higher things is for the time lifted entirely out of himself and generates a powerful thought-form upon the mental plane. This is immediately employed as a channel by the force hovering upon the plane next above. When a number of people join together in a thought of this nature, the channel which they make is out of all proportion larger in its capacity than the sum of their separate channels; such a gathering is therefore an inestimable blessing to the community among which it works, for through it (*even in the most ordinary meetings for study, when it is considering such subjects as rounds and races, pitris or planetary chains*), there may come an outpouring into the lower mental plane of that force which is normally peculiar to the higher mental.

If it turns its attention to the higher side of theosophical teaching and studies such questions of ethics and soul development that we find in Light on the Path, The Voice of the Silence and our other devotional books, it may make a channel of more elevated thought through which the force of the buddhic plane itself descends into the mental, and thus radiates out and influence for good many a soul who would not be in the least open to it if it has remained on its original level.

This is the real and greatest function of a Lodge of the Theosophical Society—to furnish a channel for the distribution of the divine life; and thus we have another illustration to show us how far greater is the unseen than the seen. To the dim physical eyes all that is visible is a small band of humble students meeting weekly in the earnest endeavor to learn and to qualify themselves to be of use to their fellow men. But to those who can see more of the world, from this tiny root there springs a glorious flower, for no less than four mighty streams of influence are radiating from that seemingly insignificant center—-the stream of thought vibration, the cluster of thought-forms, the magnetism of the Masters of Wisdom, and the mighty torrent of the divine energy.

Here also is an instance of the practical importance of a knowledge of the unseen side of life. For lack of such knowledge many a member has been lax in the performance of his duty, careless about his attendance at Lodge meetings, and has thus lost the inestimable privilege of being part of a channel for the Divine Life. I have actually heard of members who were irregular in attendance because they thought the meetings dull, and found that they did not gain much from them! Such people have not yet grasped the elementary fact that they join, not to receive but to give, not to be interested; and amused but to take their share in a mighty work for the good of mankind.

To everything there is an unseen side, and to live the life of an occultist is to study this higher inner side of nature, and then intelligently to adapt oneself to it. The occultist looks at the whole of each subject which is brought before him, instead of only at the lowest and least important part of it, and then orders his action according to what he sees, in obedience to the dictates of plain commonsense, and to the Law of Love which guides the universe. Those, therefore, who would study and practice occultism must develop within themselves these three priceless possessions —knowledge, commonsense, and love.

Theosophy must not represent merely a collection of moral verities, a bundle of metaphysical ethics epitomized in theoretical dissertations. Theosophy must be made practical, and has, therefore, to be disencumbered of useless discussion. It has to find objective expression in an all-embracing code of life thoroughly impregnated with its spirit—the spirit of mutual tolerance, charity and love.

MASTERS OF WISDOM

The existence of perfected man is one of the most distinctive, and also one of the most encouraging, teachings in Theosophy. It follows, if one thinks it out, from the doctrines of Evolution and Reincarnation. It is quite clear that if the spirit of man is steadily unfolding itself; if it comes again and again into new bodies, each in some way or other a little better than the last one; if we can see, as we do, men standing at all levels, on all rungs of this evolutionary ladder; then it is surely clear that this process of evolution does not stop with us. There certainly have been men greater in every way than any of us is, those men also were specimens of human evolution, and if they are still continuing in evolution they must assuredly still be greater than we. Where, then, are those men clearly greater than ourselves? This scheme of evolution must have certain definite stages, and it must have a goal. The probability would be, reasoning from analogy, that it has several goals; that is to say, it has an immediate goal and an ultimate goal, the last more difficult to understand, because we can see no particular reason why such a process should ever stop, but at any rate there is probably some immediate goal, the attainment of which would be the high-water mark of humanity as it stands at present. If that is so, then there should be some who have reached it, there should certainly be many who have come nearer to it than at the present time we have come. We have heard of great men of all times, the church, for example, tells us of her great saints in the past. These perfected men are saints, but they are also very much more than saints, for they are men who have achieved all that was set before them. As it is put in *The Light of Asia*, they have worked the purpose through of what did make them Man, and so they are now more than men. They are super-men, and are entering upon a higher stage of evolution than any we know.

Now the system of evolution is that the Monad, which is a spark of the divine fire, descends into matter. No words that we can use are strictly applicable to this Monad; it stands beyond our powers of expression altogether; but we come perhaps nearest to it if we call it simply a fragment of Divinity. There can truly be no fragment in that which is all-pervading, and yet any other term is, I think, somewhat more misleading. The Monad has been spoken of as a reflection of the Deity, but it is very much more than a mere reflection, and to our limited understanding the term fragment conveys more of the reality than the other. But of course one must admit that it is quite a wrong term to use. This fragment then, being a fragment of the Divine, has within itself all goodness, all perfection, in potentiality. What it has to do in the course of such evolution as may come to it is to unfold all this. As it stands, Divine though it be, it appears incapable of acting or working down here upon these lower planes. It needs to descend into matter in order to obtain definiteness, accuracy and a grasp of physical details, as it were. It must already know far more than we down here can know of the infinite, of the higher and altogether the grander side of everything, and yet it does not apparently possess the power of grasping physical details down here, the power of acting in physical matter with definiteness and precision. It can descend only to a certain level. So far as we are concerned, in this solar system it descends to the second of our planes. We speak in Theosophy of certain planes or subdivision of matter; of these we have seven, and counting from the top downwards this Monad descends to the second only, and would appear to be unable in its totality to penetrate beyond it. It can project a very small part of itself a good deal further down, as far down as the upper part of what we call the mental plane, which is the fifth from the top; it can reach only the higher part apparently of that plane, and there it again comes to the end of its possibilities. That projection we call the ego. It corresponds closely with what some people call the soul. When the ego is still undeveloped he needs powerful and comparatively coarse vibrations to affect him at first, and since these do not exist on his own plane he has to put himself down to lower levels in order to find them. Therefore, he in turn does what the Monad did. He cannot as a whole descend any lower, but he can project a small part of himself down to the physical plane upon which we are now living, and to that small fragment of a fragment we give the name of the personality. Now that personality dips down into matter on behalf of the ego, or soul, of which it is a part, and its object is to return to that ego bearing with it the result of what it has learned to do. It, as a small part of that ego, learns to function down here, to work through a physical brain; learns to act in the astral and mental body, and then presently goes back again to the ego bearing with it the capacities which it has developed. The capacity to respond to one set of vibrations we should call love, to another would be devotion, to another sympathy, and so on. It can all be expressed in terms of vibration, and that is really in many ways the most scientific way to approach the matter. Anyway, this fragment goes back again and again to the ego from which it came, bearing with it each time slightly advanced powers. There comes a time in the process of evolution when the ego has unified the personality with itself. The man then enters upon a special training, and the end of that special training is to carry him as rapidly as may be to the level which is set for humanity in this particular set of worlds through which we are evolving. This particular cycle of evolution in which we are engaged has to take us to a certain definite level. When a man has attained that level he will have reached the stage at which the ego and the Monad are unified, when the Monad can use the ego simply as an instrument, and work through it on all the planes on which it has been developing. That is the end of purely human evolution, and a man is then fit for Adeptship.

All the lower kingdoms, and the evolution, which has been going on through them, are preparatory for that of which I am speaking to you, because you will remember the ego descends only when individualization takes place. That is what is meant by individualization, the definite separate ego entering into the man. We are all at a definite stage in evolution, some of course in advance of others, but broadly speaking our position is this: Our physical bodies are developed, and they should be perfectly under our control. Of course, we know in many cases they are not, but we all recognize that they should be; that part of our evolution is attained. We have fully developed the next vehicle, the astral body, but that is as yet not completely under control, except in the case of a very few. The astral body is the vehicle of emotion and desire, and the majority of the human race unquestionably lives in its emotions and for its emotions and for its desires. Some few there are who have conquered this lower self and transcended all desires, and live for altogether other and higher purposes; but as yet they are only a few, and the majority of men are still at the stage where they ought to be working to gain control over this body of emotion and desire. The next vehicle, the mental body, is with all of us only in process of development. Intellect certainly has done a vast amount for us, but it is capable of doing very much more, and it will do very much more. Our mental bodies are as yet only very partially developed, except in the case of a very few.

Now when these three vehicles have been subordinated to the ego, the man is ready to enter upon that higher, special form of training, but it does not follow, of course, that the man who has become an Initiate has perfectly developed all these; it is quite certain that he has not, because if he had, he would have then attained Adeptship. But the man who is treading the Path must have single-mindedness, he must have only the one aim — the aim of helping evolution. When the path of descent into humanity has been accomplished, when the man has attained Adeptship, then he proceeds to live his real life, the life of the Monad, to which all that has happened previously is only the introduction. If one can grasp this conception of evolution, one sees at once that our actions and our objects in any one life can be only relative, only of small account, as compared to the whole. When a man thinks he lives only this one life here, of course the aims of this one life are the things of real importance to him, but when he realizes that this life is only one day in a larger life, all these things which are for one day only are things of subordinate account. Now such a man, having become an Adept, having attained that goal of human life, usually drops material bodies altogether, but he retains the power to take a body at any level whenever it is needed for his work. I cannot go aside now into the work, which he is doing, but we may imagine it to be very much like that which is usually attributed to the angels. The word angel is derived from a Greek word meaning messenger. The angels are the messengers of God, and so these people who are more than human become His messengers also, and humanity is only a stage through which they have passed in order that they might develop the power to be His messengers, the faculties required for such work. Most of them, as I have said, have no physical bodies, and they pass entirely away from our ken, but some of these perfected men remain in touch with the world in, order to fill offices, which are necessary for the progress of evolution in the world.

Human progress is not left to take care of itself as many have thought; it is being steadily guided, surely, though slowly, on its way; the progress is very slow, this progress of humanity through the centuries, yet it is definite progress, it is after all moving, and as it moves it is definitely guided. I know that the whole of evolution looks a mere chaos when regarded from below, but when looked at from above one sees that, however slow it may seem, the progress is orderly. The attainment of perfection is a possibility which is certainly lying before every man in the course of his evolution, and at any given moment he may turn his attention to that evolution of his and may hasten it very greatly if he will take it intelligently in hand. Very few of these great and perfected men stay behind in order to fill these places in connection with the direction of the different developments of terrestrial evolution. Out of that small body again quite a small number are willing to take apprentices, to take men who are like-minded with themselves, and train them to do the work which they are doing. Those who have already reached that level, so far as this world is concerned, are a small body of men only; you will easily understand that they are men, not of one nation, but of all the developed nations of the world. These are men who, having attained, are free from the usual laws governing humanity — I mean such laws as compel a man to take incarnation in this place or that. They are no longer forced into any incarnation; if they take a body it is for the purpose of helping humanity, and they can take that body where and when they please. It is not of any particular importance in what race they choose to present themselves.

As a matter of fact some sixteen of these Great Ones are individually known to me. I know of many more than that, but these are those with whom I have more or less come into contact, and these I find to belong to most of the leading races. Four of these are at present wearing

Indian bodies; two of them are at present in English bodies. One of the very greatest of all is in an Irish body, two are Greek, and three others have bodies in Aryan races, but I do not know what was the place of their birth. There are some others still greater who come from another evolution altogether. So that you see there is no foundation for the common idea that all such teachers belong to the one race, nor do they all live together like monks in a monastery on this plane.

What are the particular characteristics of an Adept? His powers are many and to us most wonderful, because he understands perfectly the working of many laws of Nature, which are at present to us a sealed book. But perhaps the characteristic which dominates all others in an Adept is that he looks upon everything from a point of view quite different from ours. He has absolutely no desires or thoughts connected with himself; he is thinking only and absolutely about the work that he has to do; he exists for that, and his work is always in some form or other helping forward this process of evolution; he exists entirely for that, and there is no thought of himself. Now that is so different a point of view from the ordinary one that it is hard for people to understand at all, but there are some enthusiasts, who live only for some great cause with which they have identified themselves, who will be able to grasp the idea, will be able to understand that a man may truly forget himself in this great work. Another very striking characteristic is the all-round development of the Adept. All of us, you must know, I think, are imperfect in our development, that is to say, one side of our character, one set of our qualities, is usually developed much more than the other. The Adept is equally developed along all lines, and because of that he strikes us always as a very wonderful person, because on every point, as it were, he is able to meet you, along every line he is able to understand perfectly. We are often asked, suppose an ordinary man were to meet an Adept, would he know that he was an Adept? I think probably not; he would certainly know that he was in the presence of one who was impressive, noble, dignified, but there would be no definite external peculiarity by which he could divine the fact that the man was an Adept. He would see in him a calmness, a benevolence, a certainty, expressing the peace which passeth all understanding. And yet there would be nothing to mark him out from any other good man, except perhaps the wisdom that he would show. He would be, I think, more silent than most, for an Adept speaks only with a definite purpose, only for the purpose of encouraging or helping on the great work, and he certainly does not waste his forces in idle conversation. He would be always kindly, and yet have a very keen sense of humor, but a humor that would never be exercised in a way that would wound anyone, but only to help a man on his way, or generally to make the man see a thing in the proper light. A man without a sense of humor would certainly not make progress along occult lines; it is a very necessary quality indeed. So, we might say, the ordinary man might meet an Adept and certainly not know him as such; he would hardly fail to be impressed by the man, but he certainly might not recognize his occult power.

Now as to the question of evidence of their existence, I myself needed no evidence of their existence, because I knew at once that if evolution were true, and if reincarnation were a fact, there must be such men somewhere, and it did not seem to me at all unreasonable that one should sometimes be able to come in contact with them. But for you who approach the thing in a somewhat different way, there is plenty of testimony available. We all came into this matter through the teaching of our great founder, Madame Blavatsky; she herself bore witness that she had seen many of these Masters, that she had stayed in the house of one of them, and that she had met many of them over and over again, and was indeed in constant communication with them. Her co-founder, our first President, Colonel Olcott, also bore witness to exactly the same thing; he himself had on many occasions encountered these Masters, and had seen them both astrally and physically. Our present Vice-President, Mr. A. P. Sinnett, gave the same testimony, as also our present President, Mrs. Annie Besant. She knows personally many of these Great Ones, and can tell you that she has seen them over and over again under circumstances, which entirely preclude any idea of mistake or error of any sort. I can myself give the same testimony that I have seen a great number of them, and know very closely, and if one may venture to say it, intimately, all those whom I have just mentioned to you. Many of our members have been privileged to see one or two of the Great Masters, many others have recollections of them which are hardly sufficiently defined to be brought forward as testimony to others, although entirely convincing to the man or woman who experiences them. The only objection which is made to such testimony is that we may have dreamt these things, or we may have been deluded, and the reason why it is possible to make such a suggestion as that is that the circumstances of the case preclude us from frequently meeting these Great Ones, when both they and we are wearing our physical bodies.

Of course, there are those who say that the whole Theosophical idea is a sort of fraud, and that we simply pretend to have seen these Great Ones. A great many people are uncertain about the testimony, because they say: "You have seen these people, but you have seen them when you were in your astral body, and you have brought back the memory of that into your physical brain. We do not know anything about astral bodies, we are not even certain that we possess such things, and we cannot be sure that the recollection brought in that way is a true recollection; it seems to us to be very much in the nature of a dream". But since many of us are, and have been for many years, in daily communication with these Great Ones, it would surely need a somewhat phenomenal power of dreaming, if all our experiences of this kind are but vivid dreams. Spiritualistic friends have sometimes asked me: "How do you know these Masters of yours really exist on the physical plane; may they not be, after all, spirits from higher spheres, who have somehow mesmerized you, and are pretending to live on the physical plane? "All I can say is that if there could be so complete a dominion as that sustained over all these years, then I suppose that might be so; I do not know that I am in a position to prove anything to the contrary, because of course on that theory we may be hypnotized to believe anything. If any evidence can be taken, here is the evidence of these people, and many others. These things exist, but there is this objection, that a great number of the interviews, which take place happen when we are in our astral bodies, and the Great One in his physical body; sometimes the process is reversed, when we in our physical bodies suddenly find standing beside us one of these Great Ones in a materialized form. You will say that also might be some sort of hallucination. As I have told you, these Great Ones keep themselves to a large extent apart from humanity, simply because they can do very much better and more satisfactory work when they are so apart. You must think of them as great spiritual powers, as working on the souls of men and not on their bodies. You will find that both Madame Blavatsky and Colonel Olcott tell you in their books that they themselves, being in their physical bodies, have met some of these Great Ones, also in their physical bodies. Similar testimony is given by various other writers.

I myself, for example, can bear witness that I have seen two of these Great Ones when both they and I were in our physical bodies. In one case I had the honor of receiving an invitation to dine and spend the night at the house of one of these great men who lived in India, so there at least I had the fullest possible proof of physical existence, and as I had previously seen the same Great One many times in the astral body, to meet him in his physical body was additional proof. In the case of one of the European Adepts, I had the privilege of meeting him in the Corso in Rome. So you see there is evidence for those who desire the evidence, testimony just precisely as you would get with regard to the existence of any other persons whom you had not yourself seen. But I have never needed the testimony for myself, because of the fact that I feel certain that these people must exist, and, therefore, to be told that they do, is only exactly what one would expect.

The interest for me has always centered round how one may learn from them; how one may come closely into touch with them, and be trained to help in this wonderful work they are doing, the forwarding of the evolution of humanity. We were told in the early days of this possibility when we spoke to Madame Blavatsky herself, and asked her: "Is it possible for us in any sort of way to learn more than this, can we in any way get into touch with these Great Ones of whom you tell us, can we work for them?" She said: "*Yes, certainly you can, but remember that they have no favorites; they will take a man certainly and make him an apprentice, but they will do so only if he promises to be a useful apprentice, only if he shows by his character now that he will be able to work as they worked when he has been taught; because any man who still has within himself anything of self-seeking, any man who is thinking of his own progress and not of the work to be done, will certainly not come into touch with them, just because it would waste their time to invest it in training him.*" For though their powers seem to us like those of a God, they are so far greater in every way than ourselves, and themselves are so much nobler - yet each Master's power is after all limited. And Madame Blavatsky told us that they hold themselves responsible for using that power to the very last ounce of it, for putting it to the very best possible use for the progress of evolution. If by teaching a man they could obtain within reasonable time a good instrument, one who under their guidance would do a vast amount of definite good in the world, definite good for the progress of evolution then they would consider it worth their while to invest in that man the amount of time necessary for his training; but if they did not think that the man would repay their trouble, then they would consider the time spent in teaching that man would not be spent to the best advantage.

And so absolutely the only way for any person to come to be accepted by them is to go to work and show what he can do without the training to be an unselfish and workman, to get to work on some altruistic undertaking. So long as he is working absolutely without thought of himself, and only for a cause which is definitely for the good of humanity, then such a man has the possibility of being noted and guided by some of these Great Ones, for they are ever on the watch for those who will take their places in the future. Therefore, anyone may come near to them in that way, but it is not by any sort of favoritism, it is simply by going to work and deserving their notice. The knowledge of the plan of evolution is available to us all as Theosophists; there it is for us to study, and if, having studied it, and having gained some sort of understanding, we wish to draw nearer to them, the path is always open. Be sure that we can reach them only by making ourselves unselfish as they are unselfish, by learning to forget our personal selves and devoting ourselves, as they do, wholly to the service of humanity.

ANCIENT IDEALS IN MODERN MASONRY

lecture delivered to
Sydney Co-Masonic Lodge, No. 404
in the year 1915

I think I can perhaps best begin what I want to tell you by a few personal words about myself; you will see why in a few minutes.

Though I have been a member of the Theosophical Society for thirty-two years, and have had the privilege of close association with our V.....Illus.....V. P. G. M., it is only quite recently that I have had the honor and pleasure to enter the ranks of Co-Masonry. The reason I did not do so before was simply that I am a busy man, and that, as Co-Freemasonry presents itself to the outsider at the Headquarters at Adyar, it seemed just another Theosophical Meeting with exactly the same people present as at the other meetings, except that they sat in a particular order and dressed differently. I had of course no means of knowing in what way the truth was presented, but I knew that it must be the same truth.

I hold very strongly, as I believe do all Masons, that a man should not join an organization unless he is prepared to be an active and efficient member of it, and that if he does join he should attend regularly at all Lodge Meetings, unless absolutely compelled to be absent; I held back because I did not see my way to undertake the additional labor of an extra meeting, and I did not see that I should be in any way more useful, if I came in. When I talked these matters over with the Chief Officer of Co-Masonry here in Australia, he assured me that I was in error on this last point, and that there was useful work, which I could do if I joined the Order. I consulted the V.... Illus.... Grand Secretary, and he also was of the same opinion, so I naturally expressed my readiness to be of any service in my power. That was how it happened that I came in here, in Sydney — that I have the pleasure and privilege of calling this my Mother Lodge.

I did not know, any more than any other candidate, what to expect when I joined you; but my first sight of a Masonic Lodge was a great and pleasant surprise to me, because I found I was perfectly familiar with all its arrangements, that it recalled exactly similar arrangements which I knew six thousand years ago in ancient Egypt. I am quite aware that that is a startling statement, yet I assure you that it is literally true. And you will observe that this is not a matter about which any mistake is possible; it is not a case in which coincidence will serve as an explanation.

The arrangement of your three chief officers here is remarkable; it is not one, which would naturally be the first to occur to men trying to compile a ritual. Your symbols are significant and distinctive, and their combination is peculiar; yet they all belonged to ancient Egypt, and I knew them well there. You may imagine how surprised and how delighted I was to find the old work still going on after so many ages. You have kept almost all the ceremonies unchanged through these thousands of years. There are certain minor points of difference, which I notice, but they are really only minor points.

I cannot but think that, that alone (*even if that were all*) should be a fact of extraordinary interest to you. But I must add to it a great deal more; I must explain to you what we had in our minds with regard to all this — that we regarded a meeting of the Lodge as a manifestation of our religious belief in various ways, and we held in connection with it a great body of knowledge which fits in absolutely with all of your ceremonies, and the way in which you carry out the work. And it seems to me, on looking back, that the knowledge would be of great interest to us as Co-Masons now, and would enable us to understand much more fully what all these workings mean.

This discovery interested me intensely; I spoke of it to our V....Illus....Grand Secretary, and we tried to study together something of the history of Masonry. We could see without much difficulty what must be the broad lines of its descent; hut we soon found that we needed further information about certain points, so we drew up a few questions on these points and submitted them to Him whom you call the Head of all true Masons throughout the world. You must remember that this great Master, who is to all of you, I suppose, an august and honored Name, is to your V.....Illus.... V. P. G. M., to me and to many others of us a living Man, personally known and most highly revered. I did not know until I had the privilege of entering here, exactly what was His relationship to Co-Freemasonry, as I had never spoken to Him on that subject; but when last I had the honor of meeting Him in the flesh in Rome walking down the Corso, He took me up to the public gardens on the Pincian Hill, and there we sat and talked for an hour and a half about the Theosophical Society and its work.

So when we found ourselves in difficulties over Masonic history, it was natural that we should at once submit them to Him. He most kindly and graciously answered our questions, and gave us a good deal of information; and He expressed pleasure at seeing us so keenly interested in the work. He confirmed my recollection that the Ritual as you have it here is almost entirely ancient Egyptian, but your historical setting is that of the Jewish Tradition. For example, you mourn the death of a certain Illus... Master long ago; we in Ancient Egypt mourned the death and dismemberment of Osiris, the One who became many, and we celebrated a festival at which the dismembered parts came together again, and, Osiris rose from the dead. So you will see that some of our wordings were necessarily entirely different, but the forms were absolutely the same.

What the great Master told us as to the history of the movement is briefly this. There were many thousands of people, at the time when Christianity began to dominate the world, who still clung to the ancient religions, who preferred to state their view in the older forms. As Christianity grew narrower, more aggressive, and less tolerant of fact, those who knew something of the Truth, and wished to preserve its enshrinement in those older forms, had more and more to keep their meetings secret; therefore they withdrew from public knowledge, and their ceremonies were carried on in private.

The same policy of suppression was adopted in many countries simultaneously, and therefore this retirement from public view also took place in many localities; consequently we have not one stream of tradition but several streams, so that in Masonry we are not in the position of the Churches, where there is one orthodox institution and several variants which have fallen away from the original form. With us there are several different lines of tradition, which have all equal authenticity and weight. For example, the old Chaldean religion, following out this same idea, arranged its officers rather differently, and that tradition has been adopted almost all over the continent of Europe. You will find a sketch of that arrangement given in the beginning of your Ritual, so that even there we have the evidence of two streams of tradition.

Those who have studied Masonic history know that there have been various departures from the earlier forms at different times; sometimes a new Rites seem to have been introduced, sometimes new Degrees in old Rites; and in some cases the official status of the people who introduced these changes has been distinctly open to question. You will notice a certain amount of vagueness and somewhat unsavory tradition surrounding the origin of the Scottish Rite itself; but it would appear that these irregularities have not seriously mattered, for the Powers guiding evolution from behind have taken up whatever was done and used it so far as it could be used; so that though the origin of the Scottish Rite is somewhat obscure, it has been brought into line with the higher degrees of the ancient Egyptian Mysteries, and it now resembles them very fairly. The Masters always encouraged what was good in all these efforts, in order to provide sanctuary for such of the egos born in Europe as could not develop under the cruder teachings which were miscalled Christianity. The philosophy gradually fades out of these, but the Masters take advantage of any favorable opportunity to restore a little of it.

I have heard that many people have tried to show that Masonry is derived only from the Operative Guilds of the Middle Ages; though some, going further back, have attached these Guilds to the Roman Collegia. But anyone who is at all acquainted with the ancient Mysteries will see at once that that is incorrect; because you have certain ceremonies, which could have no connection with mere Operative Masonry, but have a real relation to the inner teachings of the Mysteries. The s.....s you take, the very k.....s you use, all of them have a real occult significance which could not be connected with the secrets of the Operative Masons.

It is, however, undoubtedly true that Speculative Masonry has been purposely confused with the Operative working. We inquired about that point, and the answer of the Master was that They in the background were responsible for that, and arranged that confusion intentionally, because the Church had grown very suspicious of Secret Societies, suppressing them with great vigor. It did not, however, persecute the Operative Masons, whom it regarded as a body of men wisely guarding the secrets of their trade; the Masters therefore intentionally confused the Symbolical working with the Operative working. The effort to preserve the former was consequently successful, and They adopted as much as They could of the Operative Masons' terminology, and entrusted them with some of the secrets; these they little understood, but they faithfully carried on the forms without comprehending more than half of what they meant.

The Jews are responsible for much of the existing Masonic terminology. Moses had learnt the wisdom of Egypt, but later they characteristically tried to adapt it to their own history, and assigned its origin to their great national hero, King Solomon. They cast it into a form, which they could connect with the building of his Temple instead of with the erection of the great Pyramid; and naturally this form could be more readily confused with Operative Masonry than could the philosophic Egyptian setting. That is why their form and their legend were adopted in preference to the Egyptian or Chaldean; that is why we still mourn the death of H. A. instead of the descent of Osiris into matter; that is why certain s......s are supposed to remind us of certain p......s, when the truth is that the p.....s were invented much later to explain the s......s, which really refer to various centers in the human body.

From this knowledge several points emerge. It is noteworthy that the Masonic ceremonies, which have been so long supposed to be rather in opposition to the received religion of the country, are seen to be themselves religious ceremonies, though they belong to a much older and more philosophical religion. Like every product of those ancient and elaborately perfected systems, these rites are full of meaning— or perhaps I should rather say, of meanings, for in Egypt we attributed to them a fourfold signification. Since every detail is thus full of import, it is obvious that no detail should ever be changed without the greatest care, and only then by those who know its full intent, so that the symbology of the whole may not be spoiled.

Fortunately our ancestors have recognized the importance of handing down the working unchanged, with the result that from my own experience of six thousand years ago I can follow your ritual fairly accurately, even though the language is different. Some few points have been dropped during that vast lapse of time, a few others have been slightly modified; but they are marvelously few. Your Charges have become much longer, and I notice that the non-officials take much less part in the work than they used to do. In the old days they constantly chanted short versicles of praise or exhortation, and each one of them understood himself to be filling a definite position — to be a necessary wheel in the great machine.

It will be exceedingly difficult to explain to a twentieth century Australian or European audience all that this work meant to us in the sunny land of Khem; but I will try to give some slight idea of the four layers of interpretation.

1. It was intended as a reminder to those who did it and who saw it of the way in which the Universe was built by its Great Architect, the different degrees penetrating further and further into the knowledge of His methods and of the principles upon which He works. For we hold not only that He worked in the past, but that He is working now —that His Universe is an active expression of Him. In those days books filled a

less prominent place in our lives than they do now, and it was considered that to record knowledge in a series of appropriate and suggestive actions made a more powerful appeal to a man's mind, and established that knowledge better in his memory than to read it from a book. You are, therefore, preserving by your varying action the memory of certain facts and laws in nature.

2. Because that is so, and because the laws of the Universe must be universal in their application and must act down here as well as above, therefore the fact that such laws exist prescribes a certain course of conduct on our part; and so, as we truly say, Masonry is a system of morality veiled in allegory and illustrated by symbols, but it is a system based not on a mere commandment, "Thus saith the Lord" but on definite facts and laws in nature which cannot be doubted.

3. The work is a preparation for death and for what follows it. The various experiences of the candidate are intended to prepare him for what will happen to him when he passes out of this physical world into the next stage. Indeed I might say there is a vast amount of information about the life after death to be derived from an intelligent consideration of Masonic ceremonies. Above all, it is emphasized that the same laws hold good on the other side of the grave as on this, that in both states we are equally in the presence of GOD, and that where that Holy Name can be invoked there is no cause for fear.

4. The fourth intention is the hardest of all to explain. To make you understand that, I must try to take you back, if I can, into the atmosphere of old Egypt, and to the attitude that religious men took there. I do not know whether it is possible to reconstruct that in these modern days, which are so hopelessly, so fundamentally different.

The religion which you know best at the present day is intensely individualistic; the great central objective put before most Christians is that of saving their own souls. That duty is represented to be of primary importance. Can you picture to yourselves a religion, just as much a religion in every way, in every respect as earnest, as fervid, as real, from which that idea was entirely absent, to which it would have been utterly inconceivable? Can you think, as a beginning, of a condition of mind in which no one feared anything except wrong, and its possible results in delaying unfoldment; in which we looked forward with perfect certainty to our progress after death, because we knew all about it; in which our one desire was not for salvation but for advancement in evolution, because such advancement brought us greater power to do effectively the Hidden Work which GOD expected of us?

I am not suggesting that everyone in ancient Egypt was altruistic, any more than is everyone in modern England. But I do say that the country was permeated with joy and fearlessness so far as its religious ideas were concerned, and that everyone who by any stretch of courtesy could be described as a religious man was occupied not with thoughts of his personal salvation, but with the desire to be a useful agent of the Divine Power.

The outer religion of ancient Egypt — the official religion in which everyone took part, from the King to the slave — was one of the most splendid that has ever been known to man. Gorgeous processions perambulating avenues miles in length, amid pillars so stupendous that they seemed scarcely human work, stately boats in a medley of rainbow colors sweeping majestically down the placid Nile, music triumphant or plaintive, but always thrilling — how shall I describe something so absolutely without parallel in our puny modern times?

No doubt the really religious man took his part in all this outward pomp; but what he prized far above all its amazing magnificence was his membership in some Lodge of the Sacred Mysteries — a Lodge which devoted itself with reverent enthusiasm to the Hidden Work which was the principal activity of this noble religion. It is of this hidden side of the Egyptian cult, not of its outer glories, that Freemasonry is a relic, and the Ritual, which you have preserved is a part of that of the Mysteries. To explain what this Hidden Work was, let me draw a parallel from a more modern method of producing a somewhat similar result.

Sometime ago I wrote an article on *The Magic of the Christian Church*, in which I mentioned the Christian method of spreading the Divine power or grace by means of the celebration of the Holy Eucharist, commonly called the Mass. Who must not think of that grace as a sort of poetical expression, or as in the least vague and cloudy; we are dealing with a force as definite as electricity — a spiritual power which is spread abroad over the people in certain ways, which leaves its own effect behind it and needs its own vehicles, just as electricity needs its appropriate machinery. I explained in the article how I had been able by clairvoyance to see the action of that force; how the service of the Mass is intended to build up a thought-form, through which that force is distributed by the agency of the Priest — fortunately without taking into account his attitude, his knowledge or even his character; so long as he performs the prescribed ceremonies the result is achieved. If he is also a devout man, the value of the Sacrament is enhanced; but whatever his feelings, the strength is outpoured on the people to a certain extent.

The old Egyptian religion had the same idea of pouring out spiritual force upon all its people, but its method was altogether different. The Christian magic is performed by the priest alone, and can even be done quite mechanically; the Egyptian plan required the earnest and intelligent co-operation of a considerable number of people. It was therefore much more difficult to achieve perfectly, but when thoroughly done it was far more powerful, and covered a much wider range of country. The Christian scheme needs a vast number of Churches dotted all over the land; the Egyptian required only the action of a few Lodges established in the principal cities in order to flood the whole kingdom with the Hidden Light.

The central doctrine of the religion of the ancient Egyptians was that the Divine power dwelt in every man, even the lowest and most degraded, and they called that power "The Hidden Light". They held that through that Light, which existed in all, men could always be reached and helped, and that it was their business to find that Light within every one, however unpromising, and to strengthen it. The very motto of the Pharaoh was "Look for the Light", implying that his supreme duty as King was to look for that Hidden Light in every man around him, and strive to bring it forth into fuller manifestation.

The Egyptians held that this Divine Spark which exists in everyone could most effectively be fanned by transmuting and bringing down to the three lower worlds the tremendous spiritual force which is the life of the higher planes, and then pouring it out over the country as has been described. Knowing that spiritual force to be but another manifestation of the manifold power of God, they gave to it also the name of the Hidden Light; and from this double use of the term confusion sometimes arises. They fully recognized that such a downpour of Divine grace could be evoked only by a supreme effort of devotion on their part; and the making of such an effort, together with the provision of suitable machinery for spreading the force when it came, was a great part of the Hidden Work, to which the noblest of Egyptians devoted so much of their time and energy; and this was the fourth of the objects intended to be served by the sacred and secret Ritual of which ours in Masonry is a relic.

Our Lodges in old Egypt were strictly limited as to membership; no Lodge might contain more than forty members, and each of the forty was a necessary part of the machine, and filled a place that was all his own. Excepting the Officers, whose business was the recitation of the Office and the magnetization of the Lodge, each member was the representative of a particular quality. One was called the Knight of Love, another the Knight of Truth, another the Knight of Perseverance, and so on; and each was supposed to be a specialist in thinking and expressing the quality assigned to him. The idea was that the qualities thus expressed through the Lodge as a whole, would make the character of a perfect man. The title used did not exactly correspond to our "word "knight", but that is the nearest I can come to its interpretation.

Every member took part in the work, and the labor of those in the columns was regarded as more arduous than that of the Officers, as it was largely on the mental plane. They had all to join at certain points in the Ritual in sending out streams of thought, the object of the whole effort being to erect over and around the Lodge a magnificent and radiant thought-form of colossal size and perfect proportions, specially constructed to receive and transmit in the most effective way the Divine force which was called down by their act of devotion. If any member's thought was ineffectual, the mighty cathedral-like thought-form was correspondingly defective in one part; but the R.W.M. was usually a clairvoyant priest or priestess who could see where the defect lay, and so could keep his Lodge strictly up to the mark.

You will realize that, as everyone present had to bear his part in building that form, the most exact co-operation and the most perfect harmony were absolutely necessary. The slightest flaw in these would have seriously weakened the form through which all the work was being done. It is perhaps a relic of this paramount necessity, which dictates our present regulation that any brothers who are not in perfect harmony with each other should not put on their Masonic clothing until they have settled their differences. In ancient Egypt there was an intensity of brotherly feeling between the members of a Lodge which is probably rarely attained now; we felt ourselves bound together by the holiest of ties, not only as parts of the same machine, but actually as fellow-workers with GOD Himself.

Another point of interest is that although Co-Masonry is a comparatively recent development, its chief distinctive feature is of hoary antiquity; for in the work in ancient Egypt women stood exactly upon the same footing as men. The later exclusion of women seems to have been due to the influence of the Operative Guilds.

I do not know how far, under conditions so fundamentally different as those which exist at the present day, it would be possible to restore to Freemasonry any part of the peculiar position and power which it held on the banks of the Nile; but if there is to be any movement in that direction it can begin only in the ranks of the Co-Masons. That the body has a great future before it in connection with the new Sixth sub-race is obvious. In that sub-race, as in all the others, there will be egos of different temperaments; some no doubt who will seek their inspiration along the lines of the more liberal forms of Christianity, but also certainly some who from disposition and old association will find themselves more attracted to the philosophic Masonic presentation of truth. It is our business to see that this presentation is a fitting one — to make our work so perfect and so reverent that those who see it may find in it what they need, and may never be repelled by anything in the nature of slovenliness or irreverence. We must not forget that Masonry is truly a religion, though so different in form from that which we have been taught to consider the only religion, that its true character is often overlooked.

I am sure it will be a great encouragement to you to hear that the Head of all true Masons throughout the world takes a keen personal interest in our Order. He has been most gracious and benignant in His ready response to all the inquiries, which we have been making. He was kind enough to work His own Lodge for us in English, using our new Ritual, in order to show us exactly how He thought it should be used; and though we can hardly hope to attain to the solemnity and splendor of His working, the opportunity was a source of great profit and instruction to us. We noticed certain points in the ceremonies in which He followed a tradition, which varies slightly from ours; but the salient features were the stateliness and military precision of the workings, and the fact that the members in the columns had much more to do than they have in our plan, as they chanted appropriate versicles at short intervals.

There are various ways in which the recollection of the way in which things were done in ancient Egypt may be of use to us, for those people performed their ceremonies with full knowledge of their meaning, and so the points upon which they laid great stress are likely to be important to us also.

Deep reverence was their strongest characteristic. They regarded their Temple much as the most earnest Christians regard their Church, except that their attitude was dictated by scientific knowledge rather than by feeling. They understood that the building was strongly magnetized, and that to preserve the full strength of that magnetism great care was necessary. To speak of ordinary matters in the Temple would have been considered as sacrilege, as it would mean the introduction of a disturbing influence. Vesting and all preliminary business were always done in an ante-room, and the brethren entered the Lodge in procession, singing. The sanctity of the mosaic pavement was guarded with the most jealous care, and it was never invaded except by the Candidate and the Officers at proper times, and of course by the Thurifer when he censed the Altar. The exceeding importance of squaring the Lodge accurately is dictated by the same magnetic considerations. The currents of force are rushing along and across that pavement in lines like the warp and woof of a piece of cloth, and also round the edges of it, and anyone who has to cross it, or even come near it, should be careful to move with the force and not against it. Hence the imperative necessity of always keeping to one direction. In modern days less care seems to be taken of the mosaic pavement; I have even seen a case in which the attendance-book, which all have to sign, was placed on a table in the middle of it. With us in Egypt that pavement occupied almost the whole of the floor of the Lodge; now it is often only a small enclosure in the midst of it.

Much of the ancient wisdom has been allowed to slip into oblivion, and so the true secrets have been lost. But there is every reason to hope that with the aid of the Master they may be recovered, and that we of these later sub-races may prove ourselves just as unselfish and capable of just as good work for our fellow-men as were the people of old. Indeed, we ourselves may well be those men of old, come back in new bodies, but bringing with us the old attraction to the form of faith and work, which then we knew so well.

Let us try to revive under these far different conditions the old unconquerable spirit which distinguished us so long ago; let us recognize that Co-Masonry is a most important branch of the work of our Masters; and let us put all our strength into it. It means a good deal of hard work, for it means that every Officer must do his part quite perfectly; and that, in turn, involves a good deal of training and practice. Yet I feel sure that there are many among us who will respond to the Master's call, and come forward to join us in preparing the way for those who are to come. At present our numbers are but small; but while that is so, we have a definite opportunity of doing pioneer work for the movement.

Let each Lodge make itself a model Lodge, thoroughly efficient in its working, so that when anyone visits it he may be impressed by the good work done and by the strength of its magnetic atmosphere, and may thereby be induced to come in and help us with this vast undertaking. Our members must also be able, when they in turn visit other Lodges, to explain our method of working, and show how, from the occult point of view, the ceremonies should be performed. Above all, our members must carry with them everywhere the strong magnetism of a completely harmonious center, the potent radiation of Brotherly Love.

But to radiate this upon others we must first develop it in ourselves. We must determinedly crush down our personalities; we must weed out our dearest and most intimate prejudices; we must sink them unconditionally for the sake of the work; we must offer them up as an oblation at the feet of our Masters. The sacrifice is absolutely necessary; without it there can be no success. A brother Mason has injured you, has neglected you, has spoken ill of you or rudely to you; forget it! What is the importance of your outraged sense of personal dignity in comparison with the momentousness of the work? Of course from your point of view you were quite right and he was quite wrong; all the more magnanimity do you show in letting bygones be bygones. Consign it all to oblivion; your brain is your own, and you can force it to remember or forget at your will. Common sense dictates that one should remember only the pleasant incidents of the past, and let the rest sink into the obscurity, which they deserve. For the sake of the work, you must forgo the perverted pleasure of nursing your imagined wrongs; have the courage to take a decisive step and throw all that away boldly and finally, and make a fresh start along more sensible lines. I assure you, you will never regret it; and when it is done, true Masonic work will be possible for you, and you will have your chance of efficient participation in a movement, which is under the especial blessing and direction of the Masters of Wisdom, and is part of Their mighty plan for the upliftment of the human race.

www.ingramcontent.com/pod-product-compliance
Lightning Source LLC
Chambersburg PA
CBHW032048090426
42744CB00004B/120